heavily meditated™

heavily meditated™

Your Down-To-Earth Guide to
Learning Meditation and Getting High on Life

Caitlin Cady

For Pete.

vibes

CONTENTS

THE INTRO

HOW MEDITATION HELPED ME GET HIGH ON LIFE.

C

My own wellness story unfolded over the course of about 15 years, but I'll bring you up to speed in 20 words or less: eating disorder, depression, Epstein-Barr virus, mononucleosis, dengue fever, and the crowning jewel in my body-bashing manifestations, chronic Lyme disease.

By 21, I was battered, bruised, broken, and depleted on pretty much every level. I had some serious healing to do, both inside and out. As I slowly rebuilt my physical health, I committed to whatever it took—antibiotics, Chinese medicine, homeopathy, naturopathy, vitamin injections, IVs, acupuncture, blood work, scalding hot baths, sleeping in wet socks (yes, apparently that's a thing), GI tests, vitamin C flushes, elimination diets—you name it, I did it. But despite all the healthy eating, supplements, and treatments, the Lyme disease kept resurfacing. It was clear that something was missing from my heal-thyself strategy.

I was deflated. And frustrated. I'd tried everything. Or I thought I had. But it turned out that the last piece of the wellness puzzle wasn't about my physical body in a direct sense. The last piece of the puzzle was a major mental shift.

Up to that point, I'd derived my sense of happiness and self-worth through two things: what I could control, and what I could achieve. Throwing myself into work, smashing sales targets, never turning off, having my iPhone permanently attached to my hand, exercising militantly, multitasking like my life depended on it, keeping my hair perfectly coiffed, always wearing high heels, networking, hosting fundraisers, saying 'yes' to everything ... does any of this sound familiar? It's an attitude and a canon of behaviour that our society champions. Dream, believe ... sure; but mostly, bust your butt and achieve. Because you're simply not enough just as you are.

I'd convinced myself that my stressed-out state of overdrive was essential to my survival as a human being and a functioning member of society. In fact, I believed that over-achievement and perfectionism were not only the way I was wired, they were actually strengths (I had hustle, yo!). In reality, that way of living was making me sick. I was more burned out than a roach in Snoop Dogg's ashtray.

My immune system couldn't reset itself when adrenal fatigue, off-the-charts-cortisol levels, and an avalanche of anxiety were my daily reality. So I had a choice to make. Keep going, keep doing, and stay sick. Or slow down and be well.

How the hell does someone like I just described learn to slow down and just be? As I learned through a lot of trial and error, the pathway is through meditation.

I started meditating ... with very mixed results. I'd grin and bear it through the meditation portion of my yoga classes, letting my mind skip between my grocery list, what to have for dinner and 'Oh shit, Ommmmmmm'. At home, I'd vow to meditate. Every. Damn. Day. I'd light a stick of incense, close my eyes and listen to this-and-that guided meditation. I'd set a schedule, only to have my resolve fade away like a bad dye job on Day 5. I'd bail on my budding meditation practice, defeated, disempowered, and a little irritated.

Some reasons why I bailed, narrated by my *mind.*

(THESE MIGHT SOUND FAMILIAR!):

✻ Am I doing this right?

✻ I ain't got time for this! Got thangs to do! Boxes to tick!
A mountain of to-dos!

✻ Ugh, I'm feeling mega guilty about doing 'nothing'
for 15 minutes.

✻ Why am I even doing this?

✻ If I was cut out for meditation, it wouldn't be this bloody
hard. Must not be for me.

✻ I clearly can't control my thoughts.

✻ What's the point of this again?

It's no wonder I couldn't stick with it. I kept stopping because I wasn't committed. And I wasn't committed because I didn't really *want* to meditate. I was *terrified*.

Terrified of meditating? I know, sounds ridiculous. Like being afraid of a kitten. But on a fundamental, subconscious level, I was absolutely petrified of taking my foot off the gas and loosening my grip on the steering wheel. I was afraid that if I let my guard down and relaxed too much, my life would fall to pieces.

I was quite sure that if I slowed my roll, even for a moment, I'd lose my job, my friends and my boyfriend in quick succession. I'd balloon up to 500 pounds and spend my days lolling about in a muu-muu (and not a cute retro one, either). Without a job you can forget paying rent, much less a mortgage, so I'd probably have to live in a cardboard box. I'd never reach my full potential. In fact, I'd probably die alone with only my 33 cats and the sweet embrace of my muu-muu to keep me warm.

Meditation symbolised relaxing and letting go. And therefore, meditation symbolised a loss of control and all the terrifyingly bad things that would come with that. Without all that doing and achieving, who would I be? That was a scary thought. So my mind threw up a million and one reasons why I *couldn't* and *shouldn't* meditate. The resistance was strong.

But here's the thing about resistance: it tells you that it's keeping you safe, but it's really keeping you small. Resistance stands in the way of your growth, your expansion, the actualisation of your full potential. And ultimately, you have to make a choice between believing the resistance or breaking through it and stepping into your potential.

I didn't want to be sick and stressed for the rest of my life. So I chose my potential ...

And it worked. Meditating helped me slow my roll and calm down. And that opened the space for my body and mind to realign and get back on track. I said sayonara to the spin-cycles of stress and anxiety. I parted ways with perfectionism and that persistent, paralysing fear of failure. My nervous system found a way to reboot, and my immune system reset itself. Want some concrete evidence? There's not a trace of Lyme disease in my blood.

It wasn't easy. It's an ongoing commitment, a perpetual learning curve. But I can tell you this. Come rain or shine, come sick or well, come screaming babies, aeroplanes, hospital stays or holidays, come pressing deadlines or alarm-clock fails, I show up and meditate. I'm a straight-up meditation junkie. It's a non-negotiable in my day. That doesn't mean that my meditation practice looks exactly the same every single day. Because: life (see the list above). But I show up, whether it's for 20 minutes or just 10 breaths.

Initially, my motivation for meditating was about slowing down so I could be well. But once my health was on track, my reasons for showing up every day multiplied. Meditation has become a tool for exploring the edges of my potential. I want to be the best woman, mother, wife, friend, daughter, sister, boss, writer, creator and coworker that I can be. I want to be the highest version of myself. Meditation helps me do that.

Through my meditation practice, I've discovered supercharged creativity, heightened intuition and inner guidance, as well as the confidence and certainty to trust myself (see ya later, self-doubt). Because of this, I feel aligned. I have more meaning and purpose in my life. I've found work that I'm passionate about, and have the courage to go after the things that excite me. Meditation has also helped me cultivate more compassion for myself and others, and develop a built-in attitude of gratitude. For me, that means less anger, less angst and less nail biting. My mood is stable. My feathers don't get ruffled very often, and I rarely get my panties in a bunch (which is a lot more comfortable than the alternative). At night, I sleep like a log.

I totally didn't see this one coming, but meditation also paved the way for a healed relationship with my body, exercise and food. Long gone are regimented routines, endless cycles of restrictive diets, or battles with binge-y behaviour. I eat and move intuitively now, which keeps my body in a state of sustainable, holistic harmony and balance.

> *Meditation also paved the way for a healed relationship with my body, exercise and food.*

When I became a mother, my dedication to meditation intensified. I now have three very high-stakes reasons to meditate: my children.

For me, being a distracted mother is the surest way to a shame spiral at the end of the day. Parenting is the highest stakes (and most humbling, honouring and challenging) job I've ever had. So when I feel like I've left some parenting potential on the table, or haven't shown up fully for my kids, I'm left heartbroken and feeling like a failure.

I'm a working mother, so distractions are pervasive, patience wears thin, multitasking can feel like the only way, and presence is something that can feel like it comes at a price. At my core, I know that multitasking is a bullshit way of working (and living), that distractions be damned, and that whatever the price of my presence is (missed emails, a mountain of laundry, paperwork that gets sent a day after deadline ...), it's most certainly not worth it.

Meditation helps me stay present for my kids, and show up in the moments that matter—and it's usually the small moments that matter most. Meditation helps me listen better and deepen my wells of patience. It has trained me to remain mindful in all my interactions and experiences. I still make mistakes and have slip-ups, but the more I meditate, the more I succeed in the art of *being*. I'm a better mother, wife, and person for it.

Hopefully, by now you can understand why, for me, meditation is medicine. It changed my life for the better. That said, learning how to do it was harder than it needed to be. The advice I received was often vague or confusing, and the practical information was scattered across so many different sources it was overwhelming.

So that's why I wrote this book—I wanted to create what I wish existed when I set out into the world of meditation. I've gathered up the best of what I've learned about meditation and put it together into a simple, practical, easy-to-use and fun-to-read guide. By the end of this book, I promise that you will know how to meditate—and that you won't be bored to tears in the process. My hope is that this book feels like a conversation with a friend: honest real-talk and practical tried-and-true advice, shared with a side of sassy banter and a few wisecracks. 'Cause we're in this together. If you're ready to establish an empowering meditation practice, one that will have you feeling clear, calm, and lit the f*ck up, I'm here to help.

Let me be clear: I'm no guru. I'm not a psychologist or a scientist. I'm not even enlightened. (I know. My parents are so disappointed.) If you're looking for a silver-haired sage in saffron robes, or a professorial type with a grip of impressive letters behind their name, I'm not your girl. I'm just a person who manages to meditate on the regular. And I want to help you do the same.

'If you're ready to establish an empowering meditation practice, one that will have you feeling clear, calm, and lit the f*ck up, I'm here to help.'

This book is for you if you:

- [ ] Want to learn the basics of how to meditate without dying of boredom, spending your mortgage payment on training, or retreating in silence and living on rice for 10 days

- [ ] Have a good sense of humour and can get down with puns, the occasional dad joke, and a well-placed dirty word

- [ ] Are a recovering (or active) people-pleaser or perfectionist

- [ ] Are ready to say sayonara to stress, self-judgement, destructive habits, controlling tendencies, compulsions or obsessive behaviours

- [ ] Want to calm down, feel more joy in your days and sleep better at night

- [ ] Desire improved focus, supercharged creativity, deep reserves of patience and a sense of contentment

- [ ] Are ready to upgrade the quality of your life and live to your highest potential.

Sound like you'd fit in around here? Welcome. I'm so stoked you're here.

Big
Love,
Caitlin

CAITLIN

P.S.

Friends in High Places

Good news, there are lots of us getting Heavily Meditated on the regular. So you've already got friends in high places. Join us at caitlincady.com or on facebook.com/groups/heavilymeditatedbook

A Complete Meditation Toolkit

I want to make it super easy for you to get started, so I've created five corresponding guided audio meditations as a companion to this book. You'll be prompted to take them for a spin later as we move through the chapters together. Head to caitlincady.com/bookbonuses to stream them for free.

SHINE baby, SHINE

Chapter One.

GETTING STARTED: MEDITATION DOESN'T HAVE TO SUCK

> *'Meditation doesn't have to suck. For real.'*

As I discovered when I was getting started, there's a fair amount of meditation misinformation circulating these days. So let's clear some things up straight away. Meditation isn't religious. It's not complicated. You don't have to drop a thousand bucks to learn how to do it. You don't have to stop thinking. Levitation is not required. You don't have to go on a silent retreat. It doesn't take hours out of your day. There's definitely more than one way to do it. And despite the very convincing evidence you've uncovered on the interwebs, meditation doesn't have to be boring as shit or narrated by an annoying looooong draaaaawn ouuuuut meditation voice. In other words, meditation doesn't have to suck. For real.

Meditation is pretty magical. But figuring it out doesn't need to be a mystery.

I'm gonna give it to you straight: getting frustrated or overwhelmed and saying 'F this' is the most common experience people have when they first try meditation. If this has been your experience thus far, you're not alone, my friend.

When I was first trying to learn to meditate, I was advised by many well-meaning people to, you know, just sit there and 'practise mindfulness' or 'watch my thoughts' or 'observe a candle flickering' (yes, seriously) for X minutes per day, every day. That kind of wishy-washy advice left me fumbling around in the dark trying to assemble something I'd never seen before with no instruction manual.

While meditation *is* pretty magical, figuring out how it works doesn't need to be a mystery. It ain't always easy, but it ain't complicated either.

Let's start with the foundations of the book.

✤ Come As You Are

Here's the good news. There is no set starting point, no prerequisite and no qualification required to start meditating. No fancy apps, special clothing or expensive training needed. A cushion and a quiet place to sit are handy, but the truth is, once you know the drill, you can meditate anytime, anywhere.

Other things you don't need: a quiet mind, a wide-open schedule, or even a room with a door. In fact, meditation invites us to show up, just as we are. That means accepting that you have just 10 minutes a day to practise, or that you only have three mornings a week without your kids, or that you travel for work. This is not the time to put pressure on yourself, try to do it perfectly, or wait for the perfect circumstances. Do what you can, and the rest will follow—trust me.

✤ A Practice Of Your Own

Whatever your circumstances are, I'll give you the tools, techniques and tactics to design a meditation practice of your very own. Not a practice that you do because you heard it was good for you. Not a practice you do because you think you 'should'. A practice you do to *thrive* and live to your highest potential.

✤ I Made You A Mix Tape

This book does not offer a one-size-fits-all approach. It also doesn't include an exhaustive curriculum on every kind of meditation known to man, and I'm not going to sell you on one style of meditation. Instead, think of it more like a meditation mix tape. Like any good mix tape, it's going to take you on a journey. We'll cover five fundamental meditation techniques: breath, sensation, sound, mantra and visualisation. We'll go over a few of the benefits, like less stress and anxiety, better sleep, more resilience, heightened intuition and even that elusive pot of gold at the end of the self-improvement rainbow ... more *happiness*. We'll talk technique and we'll get our worksheet on. Most importantly, we'll sample the goods and take a few different meditations for a spin to see what feels best for you. In doing so, you'll find your Gateway Meditation—the technique that gives you a taste of something you crave and gets you totally hooked on the practice.

✼ What's The Why?

Understanding the practical nuts and bolts of meditation is essential, but how do you create a practice you can stick to? You've got to know *why* you're doing it: a clear, specific, personal reason. Because if your reason for meditating is wishy-washy and vague, your efforts and your outcomes will be, too. I'll help you discover your motivation for meditation and create your own Meditation Manifesto.

✼ Goal Digger

I'm not going to tell you how much or how often to meditate. Following someone else's prescription is the quickest way for a practice to get shelved. Instead, I'll help you set some goals that suit you and your lifestyle, and show you how to write your own personal Meditation Prescription so you can create a habit worth sticking to. 'Cause when you get a script for the good shit, it's all about the unlimited refills.

What to expect

By the end of this book, you'll know ...

* What meditation is

* How to deal with your thoughts

* Five fundamental meditation techniques

* Where and how to sit

* Optimal times of day for meditation

* The benefits of meditation

* How to evaluate and measure your practice

* Your meditation goals

* How to upgrade your practice from a habit to a ritual

* *Plus* you'll discover your Gateway Meditation, your Meditation Manifesto and your personalised Meditation Prescription.

Ready to learn to meditate, become a meditation junkie and get high on life? Let's get you Heavily Meditated.

SINGLETASKING
is the new
MULTITASKING
multitasking

WORKSHEET

MENTAL INVENTORY

Scientists report that humans average somewhere between 12,000 and 70,000 thoughts per day. But you don't need a dude in a lab coat to tell you that. Just spend a minute eavesdropping on your thoughts, and you'll get the gist.

Seriously, count your thoughts for 60 seconds. Try it. I dare you.

Part 1

ONE

Set a timer for 60 seconds and count out each thought that makes its way through the lobby of your mind. Ready, set, go.

TWO

Roughly how many thoughts did you count?

_____

Part 2

ONE

Set a timer for another 60 seconds. This time, instead of counting thoughts, just observe them.

TWO

Is there a theme to your current thoughts? In other words, what are the thoughts about in this moment?

_____

_____

_____

Download a printable version of this worksheet
at *caitlincady.com/bookbonuses* ⬇

THREE

How would you describe the tone of the thoughts? Optimistic, pessimistic, worried, calm, fearful, joyful, nervous, anxious? Jot down your observations.

_____

_____

_____

_____

FOUR

If you were rating these thoughts on a scale of 1 to 10, with 1 being not at all useful and 10 being very useful, how useful or productive would you say most of these thoughts were?

_____

_____

_____

_____

FIVE

How did these thoughts make you feel? What emotions came up for you as you observed them?

_____

_____

_____

_____

_____

_____

Chapter Two.

THE TRANCE OF THINKING: IT'S NOT YOU, IT'S YOUR THOUGHTS

HOW'D YOU GO WITH THE WORKSHEET?
SURPRISED BY HOW MANY MENTAL
TALLY MARKS YOU MADE? I PREDICT
THAT WE'RE NOT GOING TO SEE A LOT OF
SINGLE DIGITS IN THE HOUSE. AND WHAT
WAS THE TONE LIKE? I'M GUESSING
THAT YOUR INNER CHEERLEADER,
POSITIVE POLLY, DIDN'T GET THE MIC.
MORE LIKE A BROKEN RECORD WITH THE
DJ DEBBIE DOWNER REMIX ON REPEAT?
BIT OF A NERVOUS NELLY PIN-BALLING
FROM THOUGHT TO THOUGHT? OR, MORE
ACCURATELY, WORRY TO WORRY?

Repetitive and negative thoughts are standard for most of us.

Perhaps it is a never-ending series of mental pop-ups that hurtle towards you faster than you can X out the one before it: 'We're out of tinfoil! Remember to make an appointment to get brows waxed! Must send a baby gift to so-and-so! Respond to that email that's buried in my inbox! What's for dinner tonight? Pay the electricity bill!'

Or maybe it's more like the crawl on the bottom of the screen on TV news stations, a slipstream of negativity and anxiety-provoking alerts masquerading as helpful information: 'Breaking news ... totally overwhelmed by workload ... can never get on top of things ... if I make a mistake, I'll lose my job ... I need to stay late this week ... but where am I going to find time to get to the gym? ... if I miss a workout I'm going to lose control of my weight ... I can barely keep it all together ... I feel like I'm failing at life ... what if I lost my job? ... will I ever be able to start saving? ... I really want to start a family ... but what if ... '

If this sounds familiar, don't worry. Believe it or not, it's normal! Repetitive and negative thoughts are standard for most of us. Ever heard that analogy of the human mind being like a room full of drunk monkeys? Unpredictable, antagonistic, wildly swinging from one thought to the next, feral, loudmouthed and unruly. Sometimes straight-up rude. Yeah. Sometimes shit is wild in there! But I'm going to let you in on a little secret: it's not *you*, it's your thoughts.

It's not you, it's your thoughts.

❖ Don't Let Your Thoughts Brainwash You

Because you spend so much Q.T. with your thoughts, it's easy to feel like they are in charge. And that they're telling you the truth.

This is what many meditators refer to as *the trance of thinking*. We get tricked into believing that all of our thoughts are legit. What's worse is that we identify with them, believing that we *are* our thoughts. And that, my friends, is risky business.

❖ Who Do You Think You Are?

Here's why identifying with your thoughts is dicey. Say you have a less-than-joyful thought arise. Instead of keeping your distance and observing, 'hmm, that's a bit of a sad thought', you might identify with the thought and conclude, 'I'm a sad sack.'

The problem here is pretty obvious. If you believe you're inextricably linked to your thoughts, and that they're purely factual, the quality of your life is at the whim of your thoughts. If they're sad, you're a sad person. If they're anxious, you're an anxious person.

Even identifying with more positive thoughts can be perilous. Let's say you're struck by creative lightning and an amazing idea is delivered to your mental doorstep. While it initially feels really good to identify with a shiny thought like this, it's slippery territory.

What happens when you share the idea and someone criticises it? If you've identified with the idea, you will feel like this someone is criticising *you*, and your self-confidence will be shot. But if you know the idea is only a thought—and not a reflection of you—you will take the feedback in stride and move on.

❖ A Case Of Mistaken Identity

Picking up what I'm putting down? To identify with your thoughts is to define yourself by your thoughts. When it's *my* thought, or *my* feeling, rather than *a* passing thought, or *a* fleeting feeling, then it's ME. Which is, more often than not, a case of mistaken identity. So what's the alternative? Keep a little space between you and your thoughts—even the potentially brilliant ones. This helps you avoid tying your identity, your self-worth or your happiness to circumstances. You stop holding on to the drunken monkeys. You stop getting yanked around in every direction, by every whim. You're able to stay centred regardless of what's happening or what thoughts pop into your mind.

❖ A Bit Of Weather Moving Through

Imagine that you're lying on your back in a big field, staring up at the sky (heck, bring a picnic and a bottle of rosé, it's a beautiful day).

First, imagine the vastness of the sky itself. It's deep blue, open, infinite and unchanging. Now, notice a few clouds sweep through your view. They may cast shadows or even bring rain; they may be fluffy and light. Notice how whatever form the clouds bring, the sky itself does not change. The clouds move through the sky, but they are not the sky. The clouds are temporary, while the sky is constant.

Your mind is the sky. And your thoughts are the clouds—just a bit of weather moving through. You are not your thoughts; you are that which experiences your thoughts. I know, deep. But stay with me.

If we can remember that we are the sky and not the weather, we liberate ourselves, and are no longer swept about by our thoughts (or feelings, emotions and circumstances, for that matter). When we do this, there is no need to frantically search for calmer skies. It's always there, between the clouds.

'You are the sky. Everything else—it's just the weather.'
—Pema Chödrön[1]

Cloud
Passi

So how do we keep from getting carried away with the clouds? How do we see beyond our thoughts and stop identifying with the thoughts that storm into our minds? That's where meditation comes in.

Here's the good news: you don't have to control, manage or tame your thoughts. You don't have to stop them from coming. In fact, that's not the point of meditation at all! Are you breathing a sigh of relief? I *know*. Now that we've dispelled that massive myth of meditation ('You must stop the thoughts!'), it's all going to seem a lot easier.

Now you may be asking: so what is the point of meditation? Next, we'll break that down and cover five go-to techniques.

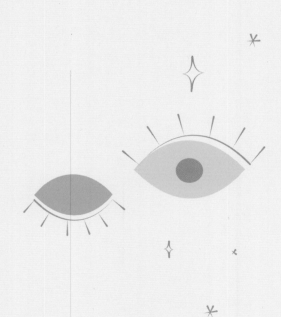

YOUR
POWER
IS IN THE
PRESENT.

Present.

3

Chapter Three.

WTF IS MEDITATION:
A DEFINITION +
FIVE FUNDAMENTAL
TECHNIQUES

Every tradition has a different perspective on the definition, purpose and mechanics of meditation. Some meditators are spiritual and others are totally secular and straight-up scientific. Some people set their sights on self-inquiry or transformation, while others are about meditation for purely practical purposes like boosting brain function. But if we strip it back, most meditators would agree that, in a nutshell, meditation is the practice of concentrating your attention on a point of focus.

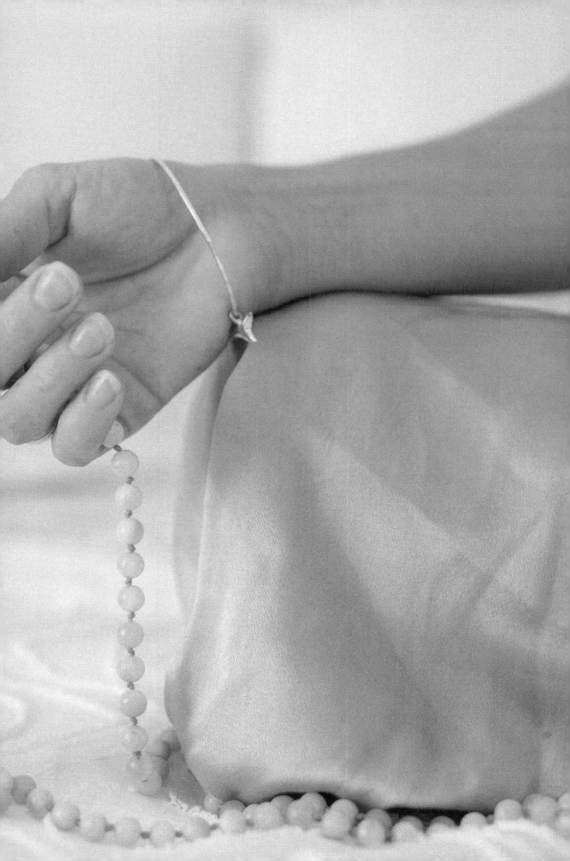

Meditation Sit-Ups

You may be thinking: but concentrating is hard. And you're not wrong. Focusing your attention *is* challenging. Your mind *will* wander. But that's all good, because the act of *returning* your attention to the focal point is what meditation is all about. This is what meditation teacher Sally Kempton aptly calls a 'meditation sit-up'.[2]

According to some traditions, this practice of returning your attention to the focal point *is* meditation. That's it. The point is not to have an immaculate, empty mind. Or to levitate. (I mean … if you've got the keys to the levitation castle, though … give me a jingle.)

Granted, some meditation traditions have deeper aims, like infusing the mind with certain qualities, or even transcending the mind altogether. But for our purposes, let's focus on this: the point of meditation is to return your attention to the focal point of your meditation.

Five Go-To Meditation Techniques

The focal point of your meditation is basically a meditation technique. So let's dive a little deeper into your options.

Disclaimer: This is by no means an exhaustive list of meditation techniques, but rather an overview to get you acquainted with five fundamental techniques. Later on, we'll take each one for a spin so you can see which works best for you.

 The Breath

Focusing on the breath is a popular meditation technique, and one that's particularly useful for beginner meditators for good reason.

First off, the breath is tangible. You can feel it at multiple points in the body as it travels in and out, beginning with the nostrils, then the sinus passages, the back of the throat, the lungs and ribcage, and the belly as it rises and falls. And then of course, the reverse is true when you exhale. This gives you various points in the body to tune into as you pay attention to the inhale and exhale of each breath.

Not to mention, the breath is rhythmic AF. This makes it very soothing to feel and hear. The tidal rhythm of the breath is as powerful as the sound of waves crashing on the beach, and can lull us into a deeply relaxed state.

Also, because the breath is always moving and changing, our attention must stay alert as we follow it. The breath is the ultimate lesson in presence. When you tether your attention to the breath, everything else falls away and you can experience presence as it unfolds, moment by moment. It's a built-in meditation tool.

Note: Some types of meditation (or preparation techniques for meditation) involve conscious control of the breath, which when done properly can have a powerful effect on the autonomic nervous system. More on that in Chapter 9!

TRY THIS: DOWN FOR THE COUNT

Set a timer for two minutes. Close your eyes, take three deep, slow, full-belly breaths through your nose. Now, begin to inhale to the count of four and exhale to the count of four. Watch the breath and simply count it out. In, two, three, four. Out, two, three, four. You can adjust the count depending on your breath capacity. Keep your attention trained to the breath. If your mind wanders, bring it back to the breath.

TRY THIS: RIDE THE TIDE

Set a timer for two minutes. Close your eyes and take three deep, slow, full-belly breaths through your nose. Relax the breath, no counting this time. Place one hand on your belly. Simply observe the natural tidal rhythm of your breath moving in and out of your body. Notice the sensation of the cool air at the nostrils and in the throat. Watch the rise and fall of the belly. If your mind wanders, tune your attention back to the sensation of the breath moving in and out of the body.

 Sensation

Sensation is another useful focal point for meditation. In fact, for some meditators, physical sensation is more accessible than the breath. This practice involves tuning in to the sensations of the body: the weight and volume of your arms and legs, the breeze on your skin, or the tingling of the palms of your hands. Body scan meditations are a simple way to use sensation as a meditation technique.

TRY THIS: SCAN ARTIST

No need to set a timer for this one. Close your eyes. Take three deep, slow, full-belly breaths through your nose. Starting from the crown of your head, slowly and methodically move your attention down your body, pausing in each section of your body as your awareness moves. It can help to think of your attention as a scanner, wand or light as it moves over the landscape of your body. Notice the sensations on the surface of your body: the air on your skin, the tingling of your lips, or the upper and lower eyelashes resting against each other. Pay attention to your arms, the way your hands and fingers tingle. Do they feel warm, cold? Perhaps you can tune in to the beating of your heart, or perceive the subtle movement in your stomach and digestive organs. Can you sense the spaces in your joints, or feel the weight of your bones? Attend to areas of discomfort or pain simply by bringing your awareness to them and observing the sensations. Take your time and continue scanning your body until you reach your feet, remembering to experience everything as the observer without judging, identifying or analysing the sensations.

 Sound

You can also focus on ambient sounds in your environment. Birdsong, the roar of the ocean, the hum of the dishwasher, the barking of neighbourhood dogs, engine sounds rising and subsiding, the swishing of the fan, even the voices of your children or flatmates in the next room—all of these sounds become opportunities for focus when we invite them into our meditation rather than resisting them.

Another approach is to introduce instruments or music into your meditation. You may focus your attention on the sound of a chime or gong, following the sound with your attention as it trails away. Bonus: Because the ear is connected to every part of the body via nerve pathways, the natural healing harmonics of many instruments, like chimes and gongs, have an immediate soothing effect on the body.

Some techniques, both ancient and modern, use drumming or other repetitive rhythmic sounds to alter brainwaves. What do brainwaves have to do with meditation? Certain frequencies, beats and tones can actually trigger your brain to shift out of the waking, conscious states of brain activity and into brainwave rhythms associated with altered states of consciousness. These sounds are like a trapdoor—allowing you to drop out of mental chatter and into the slower brainwaves where intuition, inner healing resources and creativity kick in. Think: empathy, endorphin boosts and oceans of inspiration. (Did I hear a hell yeah!?)

If you're keen to give meditation music a whirl, skip songs with lyrics and go for tunes designed specifically for the purpose. My go-to source for meditation music is Sacred Acoustics. It's the brainchild (no pun intended) of a neurosurgeon, a sound engineer and a spiritual seeker. The nonverbal songs are my favourites. In fact, I even used them as a soundtrack for writing this book! See the Resources section at the end of the book for more info.

TRY THIS: SOUND ON

If you have a musical instrument, grab it—a chime, drum, guitar, ukulele or whatever! No instruments on hand? Grab a wineglass and a spoon (yes, I'm for real). Take three deep, slow, full-belly breaths through your nose. Now, ring the chime, beat the drum, pluck a string—or tap the side of the wineglass with the spoon. Focus your attention on the sound and follow it until it fades away completely. Pause and notice the silence between sounds. Repeat this three times. Note: The wineglass won't create a sustained sound, so it will be short and sweet, but you'll still get the effects of the technique. Cheers!

 Mantra

Mantra meditation simply involves repeating a mantra. Mantras can be chanted aloud, listened to or experienced through silent mental repetition. It is one of the most popular and transformative forms of meditation, and is used across many different traditions.

So what exactly is a mantra anyway? Theoretically, you could pick any word or sound and use it as a mantra for the focal point for your meditation. Some researchers believe that the effects of mantra meditation are positive regardless of the sound you repeat.

However, from the perspective of many ancient traditions, the value of mantra meditation is not just in using a sound, but also in the particular qualities associated with the sound form itself. Repeating a mantra then awakens those characteristics within us. For example, if you're looking to burn through some limitations or challenges in your life, you might repeat a mantra imbued with the quality of transformation. The idea is that regularly repeating this mantra infuses your subconscious with its particular essence and vibration, supporting the transformation you seek by shifting you into alignment with its vibration. This might sound a little out there, but when you think about it, we are vibrational beings—we respond to inputs and meet them with resonance. If there is demolition happening next door and you have to listen to a jackhammer all damn day, guess what? You're going to meet that destructive vibration with a grumpy-ass 'tude and a headache (a.k.a. resonance). There are countless experiments showing how everything from water to plants physically respond to the stimuli around them. Put on some classical tunes and your tulips will thrive. Label your water bottle with the words 'love and gratitude' and the molecules actually shift into a stunning formation. (Google 'Emoto water experiment' for photos.) Why would we be any different? Mantras work in the same way.

There is a myriad of mantras and if mantra meditation turns out to be your jam, seek out a senior meditation or yoga teacher who can give you a personal mantra to use. To start with, use your intuition and pick one that resonates. Let's go through a few basic options together: *Om, So Hum* and *Ram*.

Om is a mantra that might sound familiar. Unless you've been living under a rock, you've probably heard it (or even used it) at least once or twice. It's in heavy rotation for a reason. Let's take it back, waaaay back to the beginning of time. Science says that the universe began with a bang (a *big, big* bang, maybe you've heard of it?), while many religious traditions believe that life began with the word of God. Regardless of how the universe came to be, most everyone would agree that in the beginning there was a sound or vibration.

Yogis believe that this *original* vibration, the primordial sound of the universe, is Om (pronounced *Aum*), which gives you a hint why it's so popular. It's basically the O.G. mantra. I won't go into great detail about the meaning of Om here (that's a story for another book). But suffice it to say that the sound of Om is considered a sacred syllable that encompasses the essence of all the energies of the universe—those that create, sustain and destroy; the past, present and future; darkness, dynamism and light; origin, organisation and transformation. Om is the gateway mantra. It opens the door to all mantra practice.

So Hum is another Sanskrit mantra, which translates to 'I am that'. It's also known as the sound of the breath. So Hum represents the union of the finite and the infinite, the individual and the universe. *So* is the principle of becoming and *Hum* is the principle of being. It's a beautiful mantra for connecting with oneness. If you're not down with using Sanskrit, the English 'I Am' is a perfectly fine stand-in.

Ram, or *Rama*, represents the fire of transformation. It is ideal for burning away what no longer serves and invoking power, confidence and purpose. It's a solid choice for new beginnings and forward momentum.

So how do you actually meditate with a mantra? My preferred method is to set a timer and rap with my mantra for the allocated time. Simply repeat the mantra silently to yourself and return your attention to repeating the mantra whenever your mind wanders. In time, you may find that the mantra almost repeats itself and you are simply listening for it. It feels as if you are merging with the sound, almost like swimming with the current of a river.

You might also see the mantra in your mind's eye (like spelled out!) or have a distinct feeling in your body. In my experience, it depends on the day. Some days I have a rich sensory experience, complete with visualisations, colours, fabulous feels and all kinds of magic. Other days, it's just me and the sound.

Another handy way to meditate with a mantra is to use a string of mala beads, a necklace of 108 beads (an auspicious number in many spiritual traditions) with a large bead at the bottom. With each repetition of the mantra, move your fingers onto the next bead until you return to the large bead, where you can begin again or wrap it up. The tangibility of the beads can help support your sense of focus. Hint: Check the Resources section for my favourite malas.

TRY THIS: GOT MY MIND ON MY MANTRA

Set a timer for two minutes. Take three deep, slow, full-belly breaths through your nose. As you return to your natural breathing pattern, watch your belly rise and fall as the breath flows in and out. Now, as you inhale, silently repeat the sound 'So' and on the exhale, mentally repeat the sound 'Hum'. Alternatively, use the word 'I' on the inhale and 'Am' on the exhale. Take your time and savour the mantra, sensing the subtle vibration of the sound within your body and mind. So Hum is the song of the breath; follow it with your attention. Like a sigh or a whisper, the mantra is soft, gentle, soothing and calming. Continue until the timer rings.

Note:

Affirm Your Way Into The Future

While mantras and affirmations are not exactly synonymous, using an affirmation in meditation is a valid technique and can work wonders. Some examples of affirmations: 'I flow forward with ease and grace.' 'I am safe. I am calm.' 'I am positive, present and peaceful.' 'I am fierce and courageous.' If you introduce an affirmation into your meditation, just make sure you keep it real. I love Dr Habib Sadeghi's instructions that the feeling is more important than the words themselves. He explains, 'the universe doesn't speak English! Affirmations are only tools to generate feelings. If the feelings aren't there, your words aren't plugged into universal energy.'[3] Damn straight. That's the best wrap-up on affirmations I've ever come across. So keep it real, and you'll affirm your way into the future.

 Visualisation

Many meditation techniques use imagery or visualisation as the focal point. Some techniques involve visualising light, colours or specific shapes, while others invite images of mountains, the moon or lakes.

Visualisation leverages the power of imagination in a number of ways. Visualisations can be used to invoke higher energies, to open energy centres in the body, to replace internal patterns and to purify the mind. Using your imagination is also highly creative. It helps you generate new feelings, imagine new ways of being and create pathways toward new realities.

People who identify as being very visual (artists, designers and lucid dreamers, I'm talking to you!) tend to *really* get down with visualisation meditation techniques. That being said, some people experience these visualisation techniques in a more kinaesthetic way, meaning they have a feeling in their body rather than a picture in their mind, if you will.

TRY THIS: SUNBATHING

Set a timer for two minutes. Close your eyes and take three deep, slow, full-belly breaths through your nose. Imagine that the sun is shining down on you, just above the crown of your head. Sense the light pouring over your head, neck and shoulders, warming your skin. With each exhale, feel the sunlight flow down through your body, saturating your cells with warmth and light and illuminating your entire body. See the golden light seep into your arms and fingers, your abdomen, hips, legs, feet and toes. Rest in the awareness of your entire body filled with the energising warmth of golden sunlight.

Good To Know

Many meditations will combine two or more of these techniques.

What's The Difference Between Meditation And Mindfulness?

You might have heard the terms 'mindfulness' and 'meditation' used synonymously—or even together (as in mindfulness meditation). So what's the difference? Or are they the same?

To sum it up: there is meditation, there is mindfulness meditation, and there is mindfulness itself.

Mindfulness is indeed an approach to meditation. Techniques like meditation on the breath or body scans may be categorised as mindfulness-based meditation because they involve bringing non-judgemental awareness and focus to the present moment. However, not all meditation techniques are mindfulness-based. So not all meditation is 'mindfulness' per se.

Further to that, mindfulness is not just a meditation practice, but is also a psychological principle. We can be 'mindful' in our lives off the meditation cushion through non-judgemental, focused, present-moment awareness. This more informal approach can be applied to our daily activities like eating, movement, working or even parenting and relationships. And though living mindfully can supplement and complement our meditation practice, it does not replace meditation.

NOW, LET'S MOVE ON TO THE NUTS AND BOLTS OF HOW TO ACTUALLY DO THE DAMN THING (MEDITATION, THAT IS!).

Chapter Four.

THIS IS HOW WE DO IT:
YOUR MEDITATION
PROCESS, STEP BY STEP

Most people meditate because they want to *feel* better. But trying to assemble a meditation practice without a clear understanding of the process can have the exact opposite effect. Clear instructions are important. (IKEA, take note!)

The good news is that the process of meditation isn't rocket science. Follow these simple steps and you'll be on your way. I've also included a few notes on how to deal with distractions and drifting attention, which are a natural part of the process. Kind of a relief to know that, right?

YOUR MEDITATION PROCESS, STEP BY STEP

1 Pick It And Stick It

This catch phrase works wonders when it comes to avoiding hangovers (pick your poison and stick with it, mate—tequila and red wine don't mix!), but is also helpful when talking meditation.

PICK IT:

Before you sit down to practise, commit to a length of time and a technique from your options in Chapter 3. Set your timer (I recommend 7 minutes as a solid starting place. From there, you can build to 11 minutes, then 15 minutes, and ultimately 20–30 minutes when you're ready) or tee up a guided meditation track of your choice.

STICK IT:

Once you've locked in your plan, stick to it and see it through.

Why is this so critical? Let's say you sit down and think, 'Hey I'll freestyle this today. I'll just do meditation on the breath until I'm ready to stop.' But then your mind starts wandering and you get frustrated AF. So you either quit or your mind tells you that this technique sucks and you need to do something else, and you shift gears into, say, a mantra meditation. And then you feel like that's not quite doing the trick, so you think, 'F this, that's enough, I'm done', or you think, 'Well, I guess I'll try a body scan … ' See where this is going? Without making a commitment to the time and technique in advance, you're setting yourself up for a wash of a meditation with a dissatisfaction hangover to prove it. So pick it and stick with it.

2 Take A Seat

Sit in a comfortable upright position. The goal is a still body, a straight spine and a feeling of being relaxed but alert. (Pssst ... we'll cover the details of how to sit in the next chapter!)

3 Start

It's helpful to draw a line in the sand to symbolise the start of your practice. What I mean by this is an expression, activity or gesture that serves as a cue that your meditation is beginning—something that creates a little barrier between regular life and meditation, between doing and being. Then, whatever happens next *is* meditation.

HERE ARE SOME IDEAS:

* Light a candle
* Put your phone on aeroplane mode
* Ring a chime or gong
* Set an intention or make a dedication (perhaps you'd like to set an intention to enjoy the process and relish the mini-holiday from doing, or to dedicate your practice to someone you love!)
* Even just starting your timer or pressing play on your guided meditation is enough to create that barrier.

4 Focus

Close your eyes and give yourself a moment to land in your body. Become fully present to this moment. Noticing sensations in your body and taking a few deep, full-belly breaths is a great way to land. Once you're settled, bring to mind your chosen technique. Train your attention to your focal point, whether it's the breath, sounds, sensations, a mantra, a visualisation—or the instructions in the guided meditation of your choice.

5 Mind The Gap

In time, as you meditate, you may get a sneak peek into the space between your thoughts. Enjoy that gorgeous gap. It might be super brief or you might find yourself luxuriating in that liminal space. For me, it feels like peace, joy, spaciousness and contentment all at once. It's like I get a glimpse into my full potential. I feel expansive and limitless. My troubles and worries are cut down to size and put into perspective. Positivity reclaims my perspective, washing away anxiety, worries and fear. An overriding sense of compassion erases any pettiness or judgements. I feel blanketed in deep calm and trust. That's a lot of good vibes packed into an instant, isn't it? Meditation gives you a lot of bang for your buck, no matter how small the gap.

6 Drift Happens

You may also notice that your attention drifts. Getting distracted is normal. You may find your mind rehearsing, replaying, fantasising, planning or imagining. You may find yourself getting intrigued by sounds in your environment. When you notice your attention drifting, just recognise that your mind has wandered (you can even mentally say to yourself: 'thinking') and then return your attention to your technique or focal point. Remind yourself that you are the sky, not the clouds.

You'll find yourself repeating this cycle of 're-mindfulness' over and over. That's okay. This isn't military boot camp, yo. Lighten up, smile at your wandering mind, and give yourself a mental high five whenever you 're-mind' yourself to return to the technique at hand, always without judgement.

7 High Fives And High Vibes

When the bell rings or the guided meditation ends, don't judge! It doesn't matter if it wasn't perfect. You got sit done. So give yourself high fives and high vibes only.

high
vibes

I've created a handy Meditation Cheat Sheet to help you keep the process of meditation front of mind.

1 Pick It

Commit to the time and technique (point of focus) for your meditation.

BREATH • SOUND • SENSATION • MANTRA • VISUALISATION

2 Take a Seat

Still body, straight spine, relaxed but alert.

3 Start

Set the timer, press play, or ring the chime. Whatever happens next *is* meditation.

GET SIT DONE

MEDITATION CHEAT SHEET

4 Focus

Train your attention to the technique.

6 Drift Happens

Getting distracted is normal, simply return to the technique whenever you notice your attention wandering.

5 Mind the Gap

Enjoy the space between thoughts.

7 High Fives & High Vibes

When it's over, don't judge. It doesn't matter if it wasn't perfect. You got sit done. So give yourself high fives and high vibes only.

Note:
On Mental
And Physical
Chatter

Pesky negative mental chatter might bubble to the surface of your mind. Don't be alarmed. Treat these the same as any other thoughts: acknowledge them without identifying or judging, and then return your attention to your focal point.

HERE ARE SOME GEMS YOU MIGHT ENCOUNTER (AND I'M SPEAKING FROM EXPERIENCE HERE):

DOUBT:
Is this working? Am I doing it right?

FRUSTRATION:
This is hard. My mind won't stop wandering. My house is too noisy. I can't stay focused. Ugh!

RESTLESSNESS:
Is it over yet? How much longer?

AVERSION:
This is a waste of time. I'm too busy for this. This is stupid.

CRITICISM:
I should be better at this. I bet Oprah's mind doesn't wander. I should start over. I'm the worst meditator ever.

You may also find yourself distracted by physical sensations. Sometimes we don't notice certain feelings in our body until we quiet the mind. First, it's important to recognise the difference between being fidgety and being in pain. If you're scratching your arm every five seconds, or tugging at your shirt, or readjusting your sitting position constantly, that's just fidgeting.

If you're actually uncomfortable, you don't need to give up on your meditation. Physical discomfort isn't a reason to quit. But there's also no need to be a badass. You're not going to win any awards for battling through a meditation when your knee feels like it's going to pop out of the socket. Simply keep your eyes closed and shift into a more comfortable position. Make a note for next time that when you set up to sit, you may need more support, different cushions or a chair to sit in.

That's it! See, meditation isn't so complicated, right? Next up, we'll explore the details of sitting in your practice.

TRY THIS: GET GUIDED

Keep in mind, you don't need to go it alone. Guided meditation is a very useful and totally legit way of meditating. In time, you might like to go solo, but there is no shame in listening to guided meditations if you dig them. I'm a big fan. Obviously, there are guided meditations galore on my website. Some of my other favourites include those by my teacher, Rod Stryker, and Sally Kempton, Tara Brach and Tara Judelle. Check the Resources section for details.

Chapter
Five.

TAKE A SEAT: HOW TO SIT
LIKE YOU MEAN IT

GET SIT DONE

Done

A comfortable upright position is ideal for meditation. A straight spine creates a clear mind. But beyond that, how you sit is up to you. You don't have to sit on the floor, Buddha-style in a cross-legged position, if that isn't your cup of chai.

The goal is to find a posture that makes you feel alert, but comfortable.

HERE ARE THREE OPTIONS FOR SITTING LIKE YOU MEAN IT:

1 Sit cross-legged on the floor with your sit bones on a folded blanket, firm cushion or bolster. The goal is to have your hips slightly above your knees. This keeps your spine straight and your energy moving upward, and creates plenty of space for the breath to move through the body. Rest your hands on your thighs or knees and keep your elbows soft and relaxed.

Hint: I like to place my meditation cushion on top of a blanket or sheepskin on the floor so my knees have a soft place to land.

2 Sit on the floor on your knees. Place a yoga block or bolster between your heels, then sit your hips back on the block or bolster. Place your hands on your thighs.

3 If you aren't down with sitting on the floor, pull up a chair. This is not an invitation to lounge and chillax in your dad's La-Z-Boy, so pick a chair with a straight back and a firm seat. Plant your feet flat on the floor and position your sit bones toward the front edge of the seat. Maintain an upright posture without slumping or leaning back in the chair. It's totally fine to place a pillow at your lower back for support as long as you sit up straight.

STRIKE A POSE

Regardless of how you sit, your posture is very important. Here are a few pointers to keep in mind:

* Relax your shoulders by rolling them back and down, so your chest is broad and open and your shoulder blades are drawn back.

* Tuck your chin slightly—not so much that you create a double chin, but just enough that you sense a subtle elongation in the back of your neck. This keeps the spine straight. (It's also a yoga technique to help quiet the mind.)

* Keep your jaw loose and soften the lips—no gritting your teeth or clenching your jaw.

* Softly close your eyes and turn your gaze inward. Note: If you've experienced trauma and do not feel comfortable or safe closing your eyes, simply maintain a soft gaze. To do this, partially close your eyelids and settle your eyes on one point with a soft focus.

* Relax your arms and elbows.

* Some meditations specify a particular hand and finger position (known as a *mudra* in Sanskrit), but in general, it's cool to place the hands on the knees. Palms may be face-up (this is a posture of receptivity, perfect for when you'd like to invite in intuitive guidance, inspiration or abundance) or face-down (great for grounding when you're feeling frazzled, scattered or up in the air). Another favourite option of mine is to rest the back of your right hand on top of your left palm (so both palms are facing upward) in your lap. The left hand represents receptivity and wisdom, while the right hand represents compassion. Ain't that sweet?

WHERE TO SIT

Do It Here, There And Everywhere

Sometimes I do it in bed. Sometimes I do it in the bath. I've done it in the car. I've done it on the beach, in the back of a taxi, on top of a mountain, in hotel rooms, waiting rooms, or squished into a seat on an aeroplane. Point being, you can do it here, there, everywhere and anywhere. (Ahem, we're talking meditation, right? Wink, wink.)

Your Meditation Station

That being said, setting up space for a Meditation Station makes it easier to build a consistent daily practice. Returning to the same place to meditate every day creates a sense of routine for your body and mind. It eliminates the need to have an internal debate about 'Where should I sit today?' and instead allows you to just get down to it.

Your station can be as simple as a cushion in a quiet corner. In fact, that's what I've got. My house is cosy (read: small), so my Meditation Station is literally a cushion atop a sheepskin on the floor of my bedroom. And it works perfectly well.

Start simple. A blanket, sheepskin or cushion you love in a quiet place. And a door. If you have kids, it's nice to have a door, ha! Over time a journal, candles or other sacred objects may find their way into your Station. (I'll tell you a little more about that in Chapter 12.) For now, keep it simple and just make some quiet space for meditation wherever you can.

High-Vibe Hangout

On a more subtle level, sitting in the same spot conditions your body and mind to drop into a meditative state once you're there. Sitting in stillness and channeling a serene state builds a charge in the space around you. Eventually the room, corner, closet or cushion where you meditate becomes so saturated with high-frequency energy that anytime you drop by your High-Vibe Hangout, it's like plugging into peace.

Last but not least, by designating a particular area for meditation, you're placing importance on your practice. You're inviting it into your home, and into your life. This sweet, sacred space reminds you of your intentions and your connection to your deeper self. So make some space to meditate.

 ## ZEN ON THE GO

Road warriors, wandering stars, jet setters and gypsies: if you're always on the move, you can make a mobile Meditation Station. A thin blanket or wrap you can spread out to sit on is an easy way to bring the high vibes to go. A stick of sage or a bottle of your favourite essential oil can help create a sacred space wherever you are by anchoring your senses.

Try This: The Perfect Perch

When it comes to meditation cushions, my personal favourite is made by Pure Prana Label. It's the best of both worlds: eco-friendly and aesthetically pleasing. The organic flax cover is hand-dyed with non-toxic biodegradable dyes, and the organic cotton lining is filled with lavender and buckwheat hulls. It's a beautiful and functional addition to any High-Vibe Hangout.

Why get a meditation-specific cushion? It's designed to give your booty a perfect perch: slightly elevated above your knees. The buckwheat hulls that fill the cushion create a firm but flexible form that is supportive enough to keep your posture on point but moulds to the weight and shape of your body to keep you comfortable. See the Resources section for more details.

A NOTE ON NOISE

Silence Is Golden, But Not Necessary

Not having access to a quiet environment is a common complaint for many meditation newcomers. But a powerful meditation practice can prevail even in a hectic habitat or cacophonous crib.

If you have kids, flatmates or noisy neighbours, the idea of finding a quiet place may sound downright fantastical. As a mother of three young wildlings, trust me, I get it. It's not always possible. In fact, it's usually *not* possible. But if it's silence you desire, set yourself up for success by picking a time with the best odds.

If you have kids, it's unreasonable to expect a quiet house at 8 am when they are bouncing off the walls with reserves of well-rested exuberance. So get up before they do and get 'er done. Or if they're in school, do your meditation after they're out of the house. Alternatively, if you have a parenting partner, ask them to wrangle the wildlings while you take your meditation al fresco on the front stoop, back porch or nearby park.

Plug In

If you listen to guided meditations, a great way to plug into your meditation is to, well, literally plug in a set of headphones. (Noise-cancelling headphones for the win!) This creates a virtual container for your meditation and puts a bit of space between you and the din of domesticity.

Come On, Feel The Noise

The bottom line is this: some background noise is almost inevitable, but you don't have to let it ruin your meditation. Don't use it as an excuse, and try not to let noise become a point of frustration. You can actually invite the noise in as part of your meditation. Just as we allow and observe our thoughts without engaging with them or passing judgement, we can take the same approach with the sounds in our environment. Rather than tuning into the sounds, or judging them, or getting involved with them, just let them pass—like clouds sailing through the soundscape.

Now that you know *how* to sit for meditation, it's time to learn *when* to actually get that sit *done!*

Chapter
Six.

PRIME TIMES:
WHEN TO MEDITATE

> *'The best time of day to meditate is whenever you can.'*

When it comes to setting new habits, consistency is key. When you commit to a specific time of day and make meditation a part of your regular routine, you free yourself from any hesitation, deliberation, decision-making and procrastination. You know it's going to happen and you know when it's going to happen, so you just do it. Over time, it becomes a habit that sticks, like eating breakfast or brushing your teeth.

The best time of day to meditate is whenever you can. That might be first thing in the morning. Or just before bedtime. Or midday. Or before dinner. Whenever. Just pick a time that makes sense for your life and stick to it. Better yet, identify the point in your day when you could really benefit from a fresh start and find a way to work in meditation then. Here are a few suggestions for prime times.

A Fresh Start

Morning is a powerful, potent time that's positively full of possibility. It's the ultimate fresh start. Maybe you've heard that saying: 'An ounce of prevention is worth a pound of cure.'

Meditating first thing is like taking preventative medicine: it allows you to set the psychological and emotional tone for your day, helping to prevent reactivity, stress and anxiety as your day goes on. Not only that, meditation imbues your waking hours with enhanced productivity, creativity and presence.

Early morning is also excellent for practical reasons: sleepy streets, no traffic on the road, and not a peep from the kids, partner or flatmates. If you're an esoteric subscriber, the 'ambrosial hours' (two and a half hours before sunrise) are believed to be the most spiritually profound. Many spiritual traditions claim that during this time of day there is a higher concentration of *prana* or *qi* (both terms for life-force energy). Meditating during the ambrosial hours therefore allows you to strengthen and cleanse your energy body more efficiently, harness prana or qi more readily, and manifest intentions more easily. I personally give this theory a resounding 'TRUE DAT.'

TRY THIS: CHECK YOURSELF BEFORE YOU WRECK YOURSELF

Nothing good can come of you checking your phone first thing. Nothing. Think about it: when was the last time you cracked into your phone first thing in the morning and felt super jazzed about what you saw? Like, 'HECK YES! THAT IS GREAT NEWS. I am feeling GOOD about myself! Today is going to be AWESOMESAUCE.' Probably never.

Dude, when you pick up your phone first thing, you don't even give yourself a fighting chance at a good day. The truth is, nothing derails a good day faster than a premature procession of stressful work-related emails, a parade of negative news, or a dose of social media–induced self-doubt. I know it's hard to resist. Because your devices and apps have been designed very purposefully (I repeat, DESIGNED. ON PURPOSE.) to hook your attention and, well, make you a fiend for your phone.

But your phone is frontin'. It's not all that. All the stories it tells you about URGENT! and IMPORTANT! aren't really true. If things are really urgent, people will probably call. If things are really important, you probably already know about them. In reality,

your emails, messages and newsfeed can wait 15 minutes. (If not, then you need to either re-evaluate your life or get your ass out of bed a bit earlier. Tough love, boo.)

So the choice is yours. You can choose to roll over, reach for your phone and 'accidentally' step into the powerful slipstream of anxiety, fear, worry, conflict and FOMO first thing. You can let your day and your vibe be dictated by the storm of input, information and opinions thundering your way. Or you can start your day on purpose. With meditation.

Meditation is how you become established in yourself. In meditation, you rise above the content and the circumstances. You establish yourself in the calm and stable centre and set out into your day with solid footing, a map of self-awareness, and a compass with the needle pointing toward your intentions. And when the time comes for you to get your scroll on or click into your inbox, you'll find that you aren't as easily triggered, or pushed and pulled by whatever you see.

It's going to take some self-control. But you can do it. Make it an experiment. Check yourself before you wreck yourself. Meditate before you check your phone for seven days and see what happens. Spoiler: Your days (and your mood) will unfold differently.

Half-Time Show

Lunchtime is a nice time to press pause. It's the half-time of your day, so if things haven't gone to plan so far, meditation can help you reset and find a fresh start. Also, meditation can help you shift out of your sympathetic nervous system (SNS) and into your parasympathetic nervous system (PNS), which makes it an ideal ritual to introduce before eating your midday meal. Not only does the PNS stimulate digestion and improve the absorption of nutrients, it has a powerful calming effect that can short-circuit habitual and compulsive behaviours like anxious eating, overeating or bingeing. (More on this in the Side Effects section, coming up in Chapter 9!)

Mid-Afternoon Mint

Meditation is better than a shot of caffeine or a slab of chocolate for sidestepping that 3 pm slump. Meditation teachers and researchers report that meditation can even be more restorative than sleep. It effectively calms the mind and leaves you feeling energised and wholly renewed physically and mentally. So why not replace your afternoon triple espresso with a double shot of meditation? It will leave you feeling minty fresh for the rest of the day.

Smooth Transitions

Sweet Dreams Are Made Of Zzzs

Evening marks another opportunity for meditation. The transition point from work or school into home life is one of the best times to insert meditation because: boundaries. Meditation signals a shift in gears and guides you to take your foot off the gas and enter cruise control. Evenings are best spent with loved ones, cooking, making conversation, connecting and winding down. Without a tool for making the transition from doing to being, work thoughts and worries often bleed into your evening hours and prevent you from fully being present with your nearest and dearest, which can cause friction and frustration in your most cherished relationships. Meditating before stepping across the threshold of your front door (or right after) heralds the end of the work day and signals the body and mind to shift from doing to being.

Meditating before bedtime is an effective way to wrap up your day. Meditation soothes your nervous system, calms your mind, and slows any protracted problem-solving, rehashing and future planning that's best left for the clean slate of morning. Plus, winding down with meditation improves the ease with which you can fall asleep, and the quality of your ZZZs.

Ready to get 'er done? Nearly there. Before we get our meditation on, let's cover the most important ingredient for your meditation practice: your attitude.

LIVE IN THE *now*

Chapter Seven.

ATTITUDE IS EVERYTHING:
HOW TO APPROACH YOUR
MEDITATION

Attitude is everything.

As it turns out, your soccer coach, your mum and those cheesy motivational posters from the 90s were right: Attitude *is* everything. What you *think* about your meditation practice is possibly more important than when, where and how you practise. In this chapter we'll cover a few perspectives on meditation that are super important to *keep in mind.* (See what I did there?)

It Feels Like The Very First Time

There's no shame in being a rookie meditator. In fact, regardless of whether you're already Heavily Meditated or you're just starting out, approaching each and every meditation with the spirit of a beginner has major benefits. There's magic in being a beginner.

Think of a time when you did a workshop or took a class in something fun, something low-stakes and totally out of your comfort zone. Maybe it was pottery or basket weaving or belly dancing. You showed up with the intention to learn and have a good time. You brought no baggage, you had no expectations. You knew the world wasn't going to fall apart if your mug was lopsided or your basket wasn't watertight or your hips didn't jiggle just right. Instead, you had a sense of openness, curiosity, playfulness and wide-eyed wonder. You listened intently to the instructor, but also approached the whole thing with a fearless, childlike, I'm-just-gonna-jump-in-and-get-my-hands-dirty sense of playful experimentation.

This is the spirit you want to embody in your meditation practice. Approach the practice with fresh eyes, friendly curiosity and forgiveness. Value the process, not the outcome. Be a proud and perpetual beginner. Every time you sit, sit as if it's the very first time.

Value the process, not the outcome.

A Practice, Not A Performance

Someone dear to me was having a tough time. They were stressed out, anxious, sleepless. I asked if they had tried meditating and they said, 'No, no, I'm not good at that.' News flash, friend: no one is 'good' at meditating! In fact, it's that exact framing of 'good or bad' that leads to feelings of fatigue, frustration and failure, and makes meditation even more essential.

Here's the deal. We *practise* meditation. Literally. It is a *practice*. We do it regularly, but it's always, always, always a dress rehearsal and never the opening night. As we covered in Chapter 3, the basic purpose of meditation is to *practise* bringing your attention back to the focal point of your meditation. Over and over again.

The Measure Of Your Meditation

As beautiful and transformative as the practice of meditation can be, sometimes—how can I put this eloquently—well, sometimes it sucks. Sometimes you'll sit down to meditate but struggle to focus. You might then judge your performance and feel discouraged, defeated, frustrated or wildly unproductive (which, let's be honest, is the *ultimate* angst for the over-achievers in the house).

And then what happens? You drop that meditation practice like it's hot. You label yourself as a 'bad meditator' or 'just not cut out for it' and toss your budding meditation practice into the Too Hard, Can't Be Bothered bin (or, for the truly frustrated, the F This Shit pile of unfinished business). Sound familiar? If it does, you're not alone.

But here's something that will flip the script on that experience you've labelled as 'bad' and instead keep you coming back for more. Ready? My teacher Yogarupa Rod Stryker put it perfectly in a lecture I once heard him give: 'The measure of your meditation is the quality of your life.'[4] BOOM.

Let me explain. The effectiveness of your practice is determined by what's happening when you're NOT meditating. Your meditation practice can feel wonky or frustrating or pointless and still be worthwhile, valid and valuable. In other words, don't judge your meditation based on the experience of the meditation itself, but rather on the effect your meditation practice has on your life.

Then the question becomes not 'am I good at meditation?' but rather, 'am I better for having meditated?' Am I calmer? Am I more patient? Am I more intentional and focused? Do I feel more connected? To myself? To others? Am I more creative? Am I more compassionate? Am I less stressed? More joyful? Is my behaviour less compulsive or addictive and more in line with my highest good?

If you meditate daily, I bet that your answer to most, if not all, of these questions will be a *oh hells yes*, regardless of whether you meditate 'badly' for seven minutes in your pyjamas on your bedroom floor or you levitate for seven hours in a cave in the Himalayas. Do it well, do it badly. Be an amateur or a pro. Do it for a short time or a long time. You aren't missing out on the benefits, and you're never doing it wrong. Simply observe its effects on your life and you'll see what I mean.

Done Is Better Than Perfect

On that note, making meditation a non-negotiable part of your day means accepting that every day will be different. Some days your meditation will be profound and deep ... even enlightening. Some days it will be long and languid and feel luxurious, like a spa treatment for the soul. Other days it will be a momentary snapshot of stillness in the midst of motion or chaos. Sometimes it will be frustrating as hell. (Special shout out to the mamas out there trying to keep the [inner] peace while little gate crashers tear up da club.)

French Enlightenment writer Voltaire is credited with dropping this little piece of knowledge: 'The best is the enemy of the good.' In other words, perfectionism can hold us back from doing something really good, which certainly happens with meditation. So make this your motto: done is better than perfect.

It's better to take meditation any way you can get it than to wait for the perfect conditions (that will never actually arise). Waiting for the perfect time—a clean house, an empty inbox, quiet surroundings, a completed to-do list, an impervious bubble of privacy— means that you'll be left waiting (and wanting) forever. Because perfect never happens. Perfect never comes.

The imperfect, interrupted meditation you do now (with a barking dog or a kid in your lap or a sink full of dishes waiting for you) is better than the one hour of immaculate perfection that never presents itself. Your meditation practice may not be perfect, but it's good enough.

When you look back on that imperfect meditation, one thing I know for sure is that you'll never regret it. It's like exercise in that way. You'll never think, 'Damn, wish I hadn't done that meditation.' So, just get 'er done. And then rest easy. Because you did the work. You showed up.

Pretty refreshing, right? Now that you're armed with the right attitude, let's get to it! Meditation, here we come.

DONE IS BETTER THAN PERFECT.

Chapter Eight.

YOUR GATEWAY
MEDITATION: SAMPLE THE
GOODS AND GET HOOKED

I haven't proffered one particular meditation technique in this book, and there's a reason for that. There's no one type of meditation that works for everyone, and if you only try one kind you might miss the chance to discover a technique that really resonates. Instead, I recommend that you sample the goods.

My goal with this chapter is to help you find your Gateway Meditation, the meditation that gives you a taste of what you crave and gets you hooked. Let this be an experiment. Sample a few techniques. Follow the feels. If one technique feels like a flop, that's okay. Keep moving.

LET'S GET THIS MEDITATION *party* STARTED, SHALL WE?

WORKSHEET

DISCOVER YOUR GATEWAY MEDITATION

For the next five days, try out each of these guided meditations and take notes. See what resonates.

You can stream these audio recordings and download a printable version of these worksheets at *caitlincady.com/bookbonuses*

Day 1: Breath Meditation

REFLECTIONS:

How did this technique feel for you?

_____

_____

_____

_____

Were there any highlights?

_____

_____

_____

_____

What were the challenges?

_____

_____

_____

_____

Day 2: Sensation Meditation

REFLECTIONS:

How did this technique feel for you?

_____
_____
_____
_____

Were there any highlights?

_____
_____
_____
_____

What were the challenges?

_____
_____
_____
_____

Day 3: Sound Meditation

REFLECTIONS:

How did this technique feel for you?

_____
_____
_____
_____

Were there any highlights?

_____
_____
_____
_____

What were the challenges?

_____

_____

_____

_____

Day 4: Mantra Meditation

REFLECTIONS:

How did this technique feel for you?

_____

_____

_____

_____

Were there any highlights?

_____

_____

_____

_____

What were the challenges?

_____

_____

_____

_____

Day 5: Visualisation Meditation

REFLECTIONS:

How did this technique feel for you?

_____

_____

_____

_____

Were there any highlights?

_____

_____

_____

_____

What were the challenges?

_____

_____

_____

_____

Overall Reflections:

Of the five practices you tried, was there one that stood out as being particularly accessible, relevant, effortless or joyful? Which was it, and why?

_____

_____

_____

_____

_____

_____

Which one was your least favourite? Why?

_____

_____

_____

_____

_____

_____

Would it be worth revisiting in a week or a month?

_____

_____

_____

_____

Keep in mind

What works for you today may not be your jam next month. That's all good. It's totally fine to mix up your practice. However, when we stick with a particular technique for a while, we get to know it more intimately. It can be a bit more challenging, but also more rewarding. Want to give it a crack? Pick your Gateway Meditation from the mix and let's use it to dive a little deeper.

WRITE YOUR SELECTION HERE FOR SAFEKEEPING. WE'RE GOING TO COME BACK FOR IT.

My Gateway Meditation:

_____

Ever wondered why meditation is so good for you? In the next chapter, we'll cover 15 reasons why meditation is medicine— for your body, mind and soul.

YOU WANT
A PEACE
OF ME

Chapter Nine.

SIDE EFFECTS MAY
INCLUDE: 15 REASONS WHY
MEDITATION IS MEDICINE

This chapter is a goodie bag full of meditation's positive side effects, but first, let's clear up what meditation *won't* do. Meditation won't transform you into a monk. You won't become so deeply saturated with inner peace that you change your name to Shanti, shave your dome and hightail it to the nearest ashram. I promise. You won't lose your edge. Or your personality. Or your drive. In fact, many of the world's most exceptional executives, investors and creatives swear by meditation.

Why? Put simply, meditation can help you shine brighter. If you're looking to invite more calm and clarity into your life, if you're ready to dial down the stress and anxiety in your days, if you're ready to break up negativity or shake off destructive patterns and habits, well, you've come to the right place. Meditation is your prescription for living to your full potential.

There are more meditation benefits than I can count. All you have to do is consult The Goog and you'll find endless articles, white papers and round-ups on the myriad reasons meditation is good for you. I couldn't possibly cover all of the potential positive side effects, so I've picked 15 that I believe have the biggest impact on wellbeing.

Shine Brighter

Brighter

Less Stress

In meditation we often focus our attention on the breath. And the breath is arguably the most powerful tool we have to change our state in any given moment because it is directly linked to our autonomic nervous system (ANS).

The ANS is responsible for all the functions your body does automatically, like breathing, circulation and digestion, among others. Depending on how we perceive our experiences and environment, the ANS responds by activating one of its two branches: the sympathetic nervous system (SNS)—also known as 'fight-flight-freeze'—or the parasympathetic nervous system (PNS)—nicknamed 'rest-digest-repair-and-reproduce'.

Reflect on a time when you felt super stressed about something, like a looming deadline or a financial issue. No amount of thinking about it would calm you down in that moment. However, intentional breathing can work like a trip-wire that triggers calm vibes. The breath can actually shift us out of the fight-flight response (SNS) and into rest-digest (PNS). As your breath becomes calmer, your body and mind follow suit. Your heart rate lowers, your blood pressure drops, and your digestion and circulation improve. Feel-good hormones flow freely. And you can think more clearly. For that reason, the calm breathing we practice when we meditate is a powerful tool for getting out of the spin-cycle of stress. In other (very poetic) words, meditation helps you calm the f*ck down and put things in perspective.

'Meditation helps you calm the f*ck down and put things in perspective.'

Change Your Brain For The Better

What's even cooler is that meditation doesn't just help you calm down in the moment. Science is proving that meditation and mindfulness actually improve and refine our stress *response* by changing parts of our brains.

One study[5] shows that over time, regular meditation can decrease the size of the amygdala, the part of the brain that signals our brain's command centre to turn on the stress response in the body. That means that meditation can actually influence the way you perceive stress and consequently, help you stress *less*. This translates to fewer freak-outs and an improved ability to keep your cool under fire—on and off the meditation cushion.

Research has also shown that meditation can plump up the hippocampus, the part of the brain responsible for learning, memory and emotional regulation. In a 2013 study[6], MRI scans showed that participants who undertook eight weeks of mindfulness increased the volume and density of the hippocampus. Interestingly, a measly hippocampus is considered a risk factor for stress-related mental disorders and is associated with people suffering from depression and PTSD. On the other hand, a more voluptuous hippocampus is associated with more happiness and may also keep mental health challenges at bay. Hip hip hooray for meditating your way to a juicier hippocampus!

Happy Guts

Did I mention that the SNS (the fight-flight-freeze response) also essentially turns off your digestive system? This is no bueno for your belly. The good news is that when you activate your PNS through meditation and mindfulness, you support efficient digestion, improved assimilation of nutrients and effective elimination (yes, poop).

It goes without saying that poor digestion can cause bloating, gas and discomfort, but it can also affect your overall health and immunity. Many ancient medical systems believe that all disease begins in the gut. And science is supporting those ancient truth bombs, with estimates that 80 per cent of your immune system is located in your tummy. Part of that has to do with the good bacteria that live in your gut, which can be thrown out of whack when you're stressed. By reducing stress through meditation, you also keep the good gut flora happy—which keeps you healthier.

By the way, if you're a bit of a stress eater, meditation can help with that, too. When we're chronically stressed, we desperately seek ways to make ourselves feel good. Eating certain junk foods can quickly stimulate the reward system in the brain. Eating can then become a pleasure-seeking impulse—a slippery snacking slope that leads to accidental weight gain, not to mention shame spirals. As mentioned, meditation can help sidestep the SNS (which leads to impulsive choices and chain-eating chips) so you can rely on the calm, sensible PNS (which gives us the presence of mind to choose nourishing food and probably less of it).

Plus, according to nutritional biochemist Dr Libby Weaver, 'when we are calm we burn our body fat very readily.'[7] That makes meditation a winning strategy when it comes to cultivating a lasting lightness of body. Hallelujah, and high fives to that!

A Clear Mind

If you never tidied up your house and took out the trash, it would eventually become a dumping ground, littered with clutter and unwanted debris. If you never took a shower and soaped that bod', you'd get a serious funk going. If you never cleaned your windscreen, it would be hard to see where you're going. Catch my drift? Everything benefits from a good tidying up. Your mind included.

Meditation is mental hygiene. When you shut your eyes and give yourself a break from the trivial chatter of the monkey mind, the endless stream of to-do lists, and the pinballing of 15 open browser windows, you declutter your mental space.

The niggling worries, anxieties, frustrations and stress become less invasive and overwhelming. Instead, you crack open a fresh perspective. You create space for new ideas to emerge. Everything becomes a bit more vibrant. Hope, joy and a sense of freedom once again glisten on the horizon.

Mood Boost

Meditation can actually pump up the jam on the feel-good hormones in your brain. The brain's production of serotonin, which is a key hormone in maintaining a positive outlook on life, has been shown to get a major boost from meditation.

And let's not forget the all-time, feel-good favourite, endorphins! You might think that the only way to get a daily dose of endorphins is to become a marathon runner. But a study published in the *Biological Psychology Journal*[8] found that running and meditation similarly increase endorphin levels. So if you don't dig pounding the pavement, don't sweat it. There's no need to lace up those sneakers to get a hit of endorphins. Meditation bathes your brain cells with a cocktail of cheerful chemicals, which makes it a happy hour you can really get behind.

Singular Focus

Thinking we've got mad multitasking skills is a myth most of us fall prey to at one point or another. As in, watch me juggle 10 open browser windows, pinball between conversations on social media, email and text, all while shovelling my lunch into my mouth. Thinking 'if I do more things at the same time, I'll get more done!' Riiiiight.

There are obvious downsides to this approach and they include, but aren't limited to: typos, a to-do list without a single ticked box, missed text messages, half-baked conversations, missed moments of connection with friends and family, rice cooked to a carcinogenic crisp, or even staring down at an empty carton of ice cream wondering, 'how did I get here?' Not to mention the massive amount of energy that's wasted every time you switch between tasks.

Scientific research shows that the perceived benefits of multitasking are ... well, bogus. A study at Stanford University found that chronic, heavy media multitaskers aren't as good at filtering out irrelevant information and have weaker cognitive abilities than those who are more likely to single-task.[9]

What's worse is that all this multitasking is potentially changing our brains. Researchers at the University of California, Los Angeles[10] found that multitasking actually causes the hippocampus (the organ in the brain associated with memory recall) to switch off. This has implications for how readily we can learn, and how effectively we can apply what we've learned. Put simply, multitasking may actually dumb down the brain.

Meditation, on the other hand, is the ultimate act of single-tasking. It gives you the opportunity to actually retrain your mind to become more singularly focused and more discerning about what you focus on. In essence, you sharpen your single-tasking skills and begin to break your multitasking habit.

A study conducted by Italian neuroscientist Giuseppe Pagnoni in 2012[11] found that meditators had more stability in the part of the brain responsible for spontaneous thought, meaning they were better able to focus than non-meditators. This ability has been hypothesised as a reason why mindfulness practices are effective in treating depression. By consciously focusing our minds, we learn to powerfully 'choose' our thoughts rather than simply react to our environment.

'Meditation, on the other hand, is the ultimate act of single tasking.'

Staying Power

When you commit to meditating, you commit to sitting for a specified amount of time. Without. Doing. Anything. By staying put and sticking with your meditation, you build resolve, resilience and patience in the face of resistance. As Zen priest Steve Hagen puts it, 'if you can get past resistance to meditation, nothing else in life will be an obstacle.'[12] Suddenly the call with tech support isn't so frustrating. You stay calm and let your kid tie their own shoes even though it takes about 10 minutes longer (and will undoubtedly have to be fixed later). You take a breath and keep your cool before pouncing on the infuriating coworker's email with a fiery Reply All. You learn how to trust the process and move on with perseverance and endurance.

Sparks Of Inspiration

Whether you're an artist, hairstylist, teacher, doctor, sales rep or full-time mama, creative problem-solving is a highly coveted cognitive function.

Meditation helps us become receptive to the creative resources that are always at our disposal by opening the channel, so to speak. Meditation reminds us of our vastness, and when we connect to that sense of spaciousness, we are able to tap into limitless inspiration.

It's no wonder that meditation has become the magic well from which the creative community drinks. Countless world-renowned filmmakers, musicians, writers, artists and entrepreneurs are rumoured to start their day by putting their tush on a meditation cush'.

Enhanced Intuition

Do you have trouble trusting yourself? Do you get stuck in cycles of regret and self-doubt? Are you always asking for advice? Are you in a codependent relationship with Google? Chances are, you're not tuned into your intuition. Which is a damn shame. Because the answers you seek can't be found on a spreadsheet, wrapped up neatly in someone else's opinion, or on a page of search results.

As poet and Jungian psychoanalyst Dr Clarissa Pinkola Estés puts it, 'over-intellectualisation can obscure the patterns of the instinctual nature of women.'[13] And men for that matter. When we make all of our decisions from the intellect (Research! Facts! Pros and cons!), we can get stuck in a whirlpool of information, opinions and, quite often, fear (shout out to you for that one, Dr Google).

The internet doesn't have an answer for everything, but your intuition does. So forget the information highway, head to the intuition *super*highway. Some answers can only be found on the inner net, yo. Meditation is the on ramp; it helps you awaken to the wisdom and inner guidance that already reside within you. By meditating regularly, you consistently receive the offerings of your wild, knowing nature.

What this translates to in a practical sense is less self-doubt and more self-trust, which renders decision-making almost effortless. When you're aligned with your intuition, the answers just come. You don't need to over-analyse and nail-bite and flip-flop and debate pros and cons and hem and haw, because you JUST KNOW. So sit down, get quiet and tune in. The answers are *yours*.

'When you're aligned with your intuition, the answers just come.'

9

10 The Gift Of Presence

Many of us spend our lives in a virtual reality. Instead of focusing on what's actually happening in the moment, we live in a cycle of rehashing the past or worrying about the future. Neither of which are helpful.

Why is aligning with the present such a potent practice? If you're tethered to the past, you live in the momentum of your prior choices, often perpetuating your unhappiness with unhelpful habits. You flagellate yourself for choices you've retroactively labelled as mistakes. Regret is stuck on repeat, and fear becomes your guiding force in navigating future choices. You keep yourself 'safe' by cycling through self-doubt and staying in the past.

The flip side of that coin is a fixation on the future. This is when you project happiness onto the movie screen of Some Day, perpetually holding out for your tomorrows when things will be perfect. When the conditions for your happiness will be *just right*. The Some Day Syndrome. The phrases, 'I'll be happy when ... ' or 'If I can just ... ' might sound familiar. But that shit is a trap, 'cause you can't mortgage your happiness on some projected future outcome.

Directing your allegiance and your attention to the present puts an end to the tyranny of regret and expectation. When you prioritise presence, you empower yourself to make *this moment* matter. And when *this moment* matters above all else, your vibe is instantly upgraded. You make choices in line with your highest good. You relish your time with loved ones. You laugh more. You pay attention. You listen. You feel more satisfied. You love more thoroughly. You work more diligently and efficiently. You're more inspired and creative. You keep perspective easily. You nourish yourself intuitively. You take responsibility for your life. You move

> 'When you prioritise presence, you empower yourself to make this moment matter. And when this moment matters above all else, your vibe is instantly upgraded.'

through challenges and frustrations with grace instead of grit. That's the power, the elegant simplicity of BEING HERE NOW.

So what's meditation got to do with it? In essence, meditation is a practice in presence. It's an occasion to notice how often we leave presence, and it gives us the strategies, willingness, tools and, in time, the fortitude to return our attention to the present moment as often as necessary. Which, let's be honest, can be *very* often. Meditation trains us to flex our presence muscles, so we can Be Here Now.

And let's not forget the impact of our ability to be present with others. As French philosopher and activist Simone Weil wrote, 'attention is the rarest and purest form of generosity.'[14]

Learning to be present with your whole self (and not off on an intergalactic adventure in your mind, creeping on Instagram, or pretending that you're listening but actually rehearsing in your head what you're going to say next) is the greatest gift you can give the people in your life. Your loved ones, friends and co-workers will feel heard and seen, which translates into deeper intimacy, trust and belonging with those who matter most.

'Meditation trains us to flex our presence muscles, so we can Be Here Now.'

Inner Intimacy

11

While we're talking intimacy, how intimate are you with *you*?

The truth is most of us have successfully engineered our lives to avoid stillness and silence. Why? Because of what's waiting for us there. The discomfort. The pain. The sadness. The anxiety. The emptiness. Memories. Regrets. The familiar jab of 'I am not enough'.

These cavernous hollows within us become apparent when we aren't stuffing them full of achievements, accomplishments, distractions and productivity. Through busyness, we get that sweet hit of feeling temporarily whole. It won't last long. We know that, so we just make our to-do list longer, overfill our calendars, keep our hands full of devices and keep our playlists primed. That way, we successfully keep stillness and silence just out of reach.

But here's the rub: the key to your wholeness is buried in the depths of stillness and silence, waiting to be excavated.

Becoming intimate with your inner life requires willingness to witness your shadows and darker aspects, to alchemise your pain into something precious and prized, and to listen to your own innate guidance system. This inner intimacy is something you can cultivate daily through meditation.

'The key to your wholeness is buried in the depths of stillness and silence, waiting to be excavated.'

Improved Communication

I don't suffer fools. I take no shit. I'm a fast thinker and a fast talker. I also have a history of putting my foot in my mouth. Being a bit reactive. Borderline bossy.

To a degree, being assertive, truthful, bold and brave is what makes me me. It's my signature swagger. But when those qualities cross over into the territory of reactivity, sharp shooting, hurtful honesty and impertinence, my swagger can turn into a limp. So how to make the best of these in-born qualities and filter out the less-than-helpful extremes? Meditation, obvi.

Meditation is my salvation when it comes to communication. Meditation has strengthened my 'listening muscles'. It's given me more space to marinate on a thought or idea before I blurt it out. Being less reactive and more conscious in my communications has undoubtedly created more harmony in my relationships and less instances where I'm left with a 'whyyyyy did I say that?' hangover.

Interestingly, there's science to back up these changes I've noticed in myself. My ability to be a better communicator has a lot to do with perspective, compassion and empathy.

And the part of the brain that's in charge of that department (the temporoparietal junction, if you must know) has been shown to increase in regular meditators.[15] Yep, meditation can literally grow your ability to be compassionate and empathetic, and see things from another perspective. It's sort of like how the Grinch's heart grows by three sizes, minus the burglary and bingeing on roast beast.

Even if you don't suffer from foot-in-mouth disease like I do, meditation can upgrade your communication. The ability to see the truth in situations regardless of your personal perspective and maintain calm vibes—not to mention supercharged patience and empathy—leads to effective communication, problem-solving and even leadership (hello people management and parenting!). If you tend to have trouble expressing yourself, you might also find that meditation helps you cultivate the self-awareness you need to speak your truth more clearly and connect more deeply with others.

I'M SORRY
FOR WHAT
I SAID
BEFORE I
MEDITATED.
meditated.

13

Better In Bed

I don't know about you, but a lack of sleep turns me into a hot mess. If I don't get a solid eight hours, you don't want to know me. But when I was suffering from anxiety, sleep was often elusive. My nervous system and my mind were in overdrive, which led to insomnia. A lack of quality sleep messed with my mood, which created, guess what? More anxiety.

'And sure enough, meditation had the goods for a good night's sleep ...'

Like many people, I was given a prescription for sleeping pills. Which seemed to help. At first it was such a relief to be carried away into a dreamless slumber at the drop of a pill. But as I learned about the potential side effects (sleep-eating? sleep-shoplifting? WTF?)[16], I was a little alarmed and decided to break up with the synthetic Sandman.

Lucky for me, this was around the same time I started meditating regularly. And sure enough, meditation had the goods for a good night's sleep, minus any freaky nocturnal behaviour. Meditation helps me fall asleep more easily and sleep better, so I wake up fresh.

It's not just me that's getting better in the sack.
A randomised clinical trial conducted at the University
of Southern California[17] showed some interesting results
regarding sleep and meditation. The study was conducted
with a small group of middle-aged and older adults who
had trouble sleeping. It found that those who practised
mindfulness meditation for six weeks reported less
insomnia and fatigue, and improved sleep quality. Sleep
issues are often associated with depression, so it's no
surprise that participants also experienced positive
outcomes for mood.

So how come meditators in the study got better shut-eye?
Mindfulness meditation is one way of triggering what
Dr Herbert Benson, Director Emeritus of the Harvard-
affiliated Benson-Henry Institute for Mind Body Medicine,
first called the 'relaxation response'. Remember our old
friend the parasympathetic nervous system? Yep, bringing
the PNS online helps us sleep better, too.

Through regular meditation, you build your ability to trigger
the relaxation response, and, in time, relaxation becomes
more like a reflex. Which is a nice option to have when
you're staring down the barrel of eight hours of alone time
in the dark with your anxiety.

'Through regular meditation, you build your ability to trigger the relaxation response, and, in time, relaxation becomes more like a reflex.'

Feeling All The Feels

Speaking of being alone with your feelings, sometimes it's challenging to sit with reality. Human beings are biologically wired to move away from pain and toward pleasure. So when you're in pain, feel confronted, or are even just uncomfortable, it's normal to concoct exit strategies to take you away from those sensations.

The type of escape ranges from getting lost in virtual realities (*I see you scrollin'* ...) to numbing out with addictions (drugs, alcohol, sugar, sex, shopping or even overexercise, to name a few). We can also become overly identified with pleasure and become fixated on feeling good fast, which can evolve into compulsive tendencies (ménage à trois with Ben & Jerry anyone?).

Obviously, avoiding our feelings isn't a useful strategy and it always comes back to bite us in the ass. But at the same time, we don't need to identify with them. Just as we don't get caught up with our thoughts (clouds passing in the sky, right?), we don't binge on bad vibes. We let the feeling come, and then we let it go.

This, my friends, is the art of *equanimity*, a word derived from the Latin *aequus* and *animus*, which translate to 'balanced' and 'internal state' respectively. In plain English: equanimity is even-mindedness.

Practising equanimity in meditation allows us to cultivate equanimity in our daily lives. By sitting still and noticing the changing landscape of emotions and thoughts in meditation, we practise *staying* (rather than leaving or resisting) and *listening* (without judgement or attachment).

Equanimity is the art of staying. And it's an art that's worth devoting yourself to. Whether in a moment of pleasure or pain, you'll be surprised how much peace you will experience just by giving yourself permission to *feel all the feels*.

Be warned, as you become an expert in the art of equanimity, you'll probably need to let Ben & Jerry know that the love triangle is over. Drama queens might find themselves abdicating their thrones. And you might even cancel your memberships to the Guilt Trip Frequent Flyer Club *and* the Shame Spiral Society. It's that transformative.

15 Good Habits

I've touched on this in quite a few of the preceding sections, but just to be clear, I believe that a regular meditation practice is a useful tool for overcoming harmful habits like eating disorders, addictions, cutting, over-achievement, perfectionism, gossip, social media obsessions and other self-destructive behaviours.

Consider some of the meditation benefits we've just gone over: soothing the nervous system, decreasing stress and creating calm. Increased patience, resolve and resilience. Non-judgement, non-attachment and presence. Equanimity. Learning to honour our feelings without attaching to them. A deeper connection to our intuitive self.

This combination of qualities and skills will equip you to naturally replace negative habits with healthier behaviours. Through the improved self-awareness and compassion that arises from meditation, you can even begin to unravel the reason you're self-soothing in the first place—eliminating the very root of a harmful habit for good.

'This combination of qualities and skills will equip you to naturally replace negative habits with healthier behaviours.'

I could go on,
but I'd rather be
meditating. Now
that you know the
reasons why you
should meditate,
let's get you clear
on why you *will*.
It's time to unlock
your personal
motivation for
meditation.

Note:
SEEK SUPPORT IF YOU NEED IT

I've talked a lot about how meditation has helped me heal because that's been my experience. I have not experienced anything but positive side effects from meditation. However, for some people, meditation may be destabilising. If you experience emotional or psychological disturbances or just feel you need support to keep yourself safe and well, I encourage you to seek out the guidance of a credible senior teacher or psychologist trained in mindfulness or meditation techniques, or to seek the advice of a medical doctor before continuing a practice.

Chapter Ten.

MEDITATION MOTIVATION: THE WHY MATTERS

Most people dip their toe into the meditation pool because they've heard it's good for this-and-that. Maybe it starts with advice from an expert, a convincing piece of clinical evidence, a testimonial from a friend or tips in a self-help book. Suddenly they feel like it's something they *should* try.

But if you launch your meditation practice with a flimsy 'I heard it's good for stress' or, worse, no real reason at all, you're shooting yourself in the foot. Because if your reasons for meditating are wishy-washy and vague, your efforts and outcomes will be, too.

The best reason to meditate comes from within. An honest, compelling and clearly articulated personal reason *why* you're putting your tush on the meditation cush' is the lynchpin for a lasting, meaningful practice.

Give Your Practice Purpose

Investing your time and energy in something is easy when you know the reason. Identifying a clear personal purpose for your practice is self-motivating. It inspires you to *start* showing up and serves as a touchstone that motivates you to *keep* showing up. And it's that inspiration and motivation that turns a cheap flirtation with meditation into a committed relationship.

Once you're clear on your purpose, getting Heavily Meditated on the regular will become a non-negotiable, and even something you look forward to.

LISTEN UP:

You may want to skip ahead. But don't. Stay right here. Don't look away. This is the point of transformation. How you engage with this section of the book has the potential to make or break your meditation practice.

Light And Shadow

The most powerful and compelling motivation for meditating is usually a combination of light and dark.

The light aspect is what matters most. It's the wholesome desire to live in alignment with your values—who and what is most important to you. Living in alignment with your values makes life feel meaningful and fulfilling, and primes you to live to your full potential. And in my book, there's no greater high than that.

The shadow aspect represents the thoughts and behaviours that are out of alignment with your values and that you'd like to release. These include inner experiences like limiting beliefs and negative feelings, as well as outer experiences like habits you use to avoid or soothe negative inner experiences.

How To Get High On Life

The following worksheet takes you through a powerful eight-step process. You'll get crystal clear about your big-picture values and where your thoughts and behaviours might be out of alignment. You'll understand what actions you can take to live in alignment with what matters most. You'll craft an affirmation for your future, and therein discover your purpose for meditating—your Meditation Manifesto, which will help you stay on track and get those high-on-life feels on tap.

WORKSHEET
A MAP TO WHAT MATTERS MOST

Part 1:

IDENTIFYING YOUR VALUES, BELIEFS AND BEHAVIOURS

This exercise draws from the ACT Matrix, which was originally created by Dr Kevin Polk.[18]

Use the map on page 169 to fill in your answers to the next four questions. This is a powerful, tangible way to see how you're moving toward or away from what you value most. Throughout the worksheet, I share aspects of my story to serve as inspiration for your own process.

P.S. Download a printable version at *caitlincady.com/bookbonuses*

1. Values: Who + What Matters

Who is important to me? What matters most to me? What or who lights me up and makes me feel most alive, joyful or fulfilled?

NOTE:

If you come up with a huge list here, that's totally cool. Once you've done a brain dump, just pick the one that's most important to you right now and work through questions 2 to 8 with that single value. You can repeat the process as many times as you like, but it's simplest to work with one value at a time. You may work with a priority value for a few months, until it flows effortlessly, and then repeat this process with another value and switch up your Meditation Manifesto!

2. Inner Experience: What Gets In The Way

What thoughts, feelings, stories or beliefs get in the way of who and what matters most to me?

MY STORY:

One of the things that matters most to me is my family, obviously. But over-achievement and perfectionism are shadows I still dance with to this day, and they can actually affect the way I engage with my family. An example of a thought or story that can move me away from connecting fully with my family is 'I am not enough'.

3. Outer Experience: The Things You Do

What behaviours or actions do I do to move away from those thoughts, feelings, stories or beliefs?

When I do this behaviour, does it get rid of the feeling/thought/story? If so, for how long?

What do I do when the feeling/thought/story returns?

MY STORY:

The behaviour that temporarily soothes my sense of not-enoughness is to fill every waking moment with productivity—constantly doing, ticking boxes and chasing achievements big and small. This behaviour moves me away from what matters most because it prevents me from being fully present with my family. This behaviour makes me feel good in the short term, but when the not-enoughness resurfaces, the impulse is to DO more, which takes me away from my family again. See the cycle here?

NOTE: NO GUILT TRIPS HERE!

Don't fret if you find yourself returning to the same behaviour over and over again! It's totally normal to get stuck in a loop. For example, you feel anxious, so you might drink a little too much wine a little too often. The wine offers you temporary relief, but the anxious feelings resurface when the buzz wears off. So then the next night you might find yourself pouring another glass of wine ... and so on.

The truth is, these 'negative' behaviours or habits serve a positive purpose! So rather than giving yourself a guilt trip about your less-than-helpful habits, recognise them as clues about where your behaviours are out of alignment with your values, and why. Think about it: you're not drinking to make yourself feel like shit. You're reaching for relief. All humans instinctively look for solutions to soothe pain. At some stage it may have been helpful to have a wine to take the edge off, but over time it may have become a form of self-medication and habitual escape. When you're ready, recognising these stuck cycles of beliefs and behaviours offers you an opportunity to understand the pain you're trying to soothe, reset your habits, and choose a different behaviour that moves you toward what matters most, rather than away from it.

4. Forward Movement

What behaviours or actions could I do to move toward alignment and valuing what's important to me?

Jot down what you already do, what you'd like to do more of, as well as new things you could do.

My actions for forward movement include: creating boundaries around my time and how I use it, such as working within set hours; turning my phone on silent or putting it in a cupboard in the evening; having dedicated one-on-one time with the kids (we call it 'heart-to-heart time') where they choose what we do (and no laundry gets folded, no dishwashers unloaded, and no meals cooked); single-tasking without exception; and taking a breath to reflect before I say 'yes' to new work and volunteer requests.

A Map To What Matters Most

Outer Experience

BEHAVIOURS • ACTIONS

3.

What behaviours or actions do I do to move
away from those thoughts, feelings, stories
or beliefs? When I do this behaviour, does it
get rid of the feeling/thought/story?
If so, for how long?

4.

What behaviours or actions
could I do to move toward what's
important to me?

AWAY FROM WHAT MATTERS

TOWARD WHAT MATTERS

2.

What thoughts, feelings, stories or
beliefs get in the way of who and what
matters most to me?

1.

Who is important to me?
What matters most?

Inner Experience

THOUGHTS, FEELINGS, BELIEFS

Part 2:

DIRECTION & FUTURE INTENTION

5. Reflection On Your Direction

In the last 24 hours, roughly how many hours did I spend acting in ways that moved me toward who and what matters most to me? And how many hours did I spend acting in ways that moved me away from who and what matters most?

_____ hours moving toward + _____ hours moving away = 24 hours total

NOTE:

This is a really useful benchmark and we'll refer back to it when we talk about meditation journalling in the Track Star section in Chapter 11!

6. Affirm The Future Feels

If I spent more time acting in ways that moved me toward who and what matters most to me, how would I feel? What would change? What would life look and feel like? How would I be in alignment with what matters most to me?

_____
_____
_____
_____
_____
_____
_____
_____
_____
_____
_____
_____
_____
_____
_____
_____
_____
_____

Write an affirmative phrase that gets to the heart of those future feels:

_____
_____
_____

MY STORY:

I am fully present, creating deep and satisfying connections with my family; I am enough, just as I am.

OTHER EXAMPLES:

I create and share courageously; I am enough; I am well-rested and calm; I am vibrant, nourished, healthy and well; I am free to be myself, and I trust myself completely.

7. Behaviour Booster

In what ways could meditation help support me in making this affirmation a reality?

_____
_____
_____
_____
_____
_____
_____
_____
_____
_____
_____
_____
_____
_____
_____
_____

Feel free to refer back to the Side Effects in Chapter 9. You might also find it useful to refer to your answers from #4 (page 167), as some of these actions and behaviours may be directly supported by meditation. For example, if feeling more rested and calm is important to you, improving your sleep hygiene may be a behaviour that moves you toward that. Meditation can help you unwind at the end of the day, decrease insomnia and support a better night's sleep.

MY STORY:

Meditation helps me connect deeply with myself, and reminds me of my vastness and inherent wholeness. When I meditate between work and family life, it helps me to transition from doing into being. Meditation makes me feel less stressed and helps me keep things in perspective so I can remember what really matters and what is not actually urgent or important. Meditation teaches me how to focus my attention and single-task, so that when I'm working, I'm powerfully efficient, and when I'm playing, I'm free to be joyful and have fun without worrying about what needs doing. Meditation helps me feel more calm, relaxed, focused and present so I can give my kids the best of me. Meditation helps me stay stress-free, healthy and well.

8. Meditation Manifesto

Refer to your affirmation #6 (page 171). This is the heart of what matters most to you, which is the very best reason for meditating. Let's rephrase your affirmation into an empowering Meditation Manifesto. Your manifesto is a reminder of *why* you are meditating. It's also a signpost pointing you toward what matters most so you can live in alignment with your values and get high on life.

'Your manifesto is a reminder of why you are meditating.'

MY STORY:

I meditate to remember my wholeness and the graceful ease of being. I meditate to show up fully present in every moment possible and to deeply connect with myself and the people I love.

OTHER EXAMPLES:

I meditate to stay connected to the boundless creativity and confidence within me; I meditate to remember that it's safe to transition out of doing and into being; I meditate so that I can relax, unwind and sleep well; I meditate to support nourishing choices in line with my highest good; I meditate to connect with my intuition and inner guidance so that I can make decisions with ease.

MY MEDITATION MANIFESTO:

_____
_____
_____
_____
_____
_____

WOOHOO!
YOU DID IT!
Nice work

Next up, we're talking goal setting and how to become a straight-up meditation junkie.

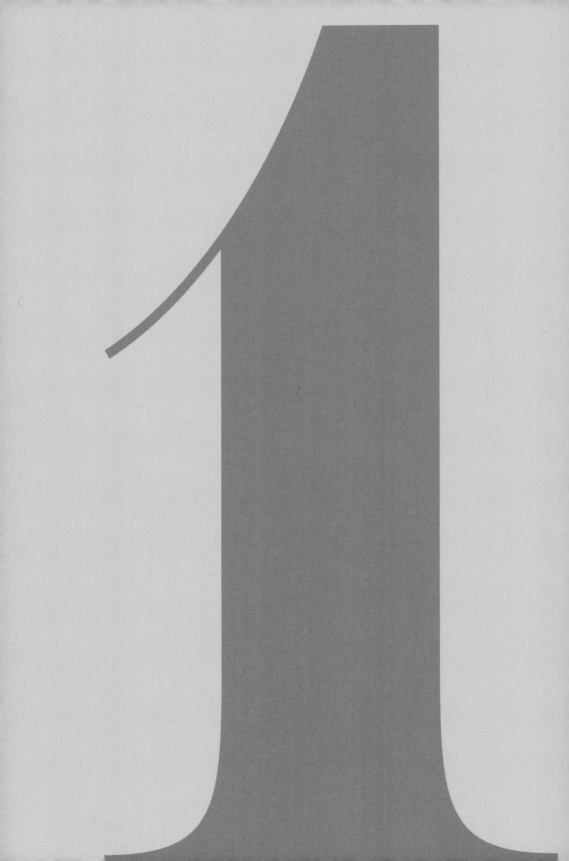

Chapter Eleven.

GET SIT DONE: SET GOALS
AND MAKE MEDITATION A
HABIT THAT STICKS

YOUR MEDITATION MANIFESTO IS NAILED DOWN, AND NOW IT'S TIME TO SET SOME GOALS. **DEFINING YOUR PERSONAL STARTING POINT, SETTING THE RIGHT GOALS FOR YOU, AND RIGGING THE GAME SO YOU CAN WIN IT** ARE THE SECRETS TO GETTING SIT DONE ON THE REGULAR AND MAKING MEDITATION A HABIT THAT STICKS. PLUS, WE'LL COVER THREE DIFFERENT WAYS YOU CAN TRACK YOUR PROGRESS.

HIT

MUTE

ON SELF

DOUBT

baby.

Come As You Are, Start Where You Are

First off, hear this: meditation is not a competition, yo! In the Western cultural framework, we've managed to turn everything into a competitive sport, even our personal practices. Whether it's yoga or meditation, many people are too intimidated to try because they think they aren't 'good enough' or they aren't 'ready'. In the context of yoga, I often hear people say, 'I'm going to start going to a class when I'm more flexible ... or when I lose five kilos'. In the context of meditation, I hear 'my mind won't stop thinking' or 'I'm not good at meditation' or 'I don't have time'. What this tells me is that most people have a perception that there are general prerequisites for what are *purely* personal practices.

But there is no prerequisite or qualification required to start meditating. In fact, meditation invites you to show up just as you are. Meditation is inclusive and open to all. You don't need to be religious, spiritual or even have a calm mind or an hour to spare. You just need to start where you are. Kids, dogs, jobs, busy minds and tight schedules welcome.

You just need to start where you are.

Rig The Game So You Can Win It

When you start where you are, then you can set meditation goals you can actually reach. A meditation practice that works, and that will make a real difference in your life, doesn't need to be 45 or 60 minutes a day, particularly if you're just getting started. So rather than overcommitting, getting overwhelmed, and then walking away, do just the opposite. Set yourself a really achievable schedule. The seven-minute meditation you actually *do* will benefit you more than the 30-minute meditation you never get to. As uber-entrepreneur Tim Ferriss puts it: 'rig the game so you can win it.'[19]

By purposely creating a realistic and achievable schedule, you set yourself up to actually get 'er done. Ferriss explains that this way of setting goals essentially alleviates performance anxiety, and 'allows you to overshoot that goal, continually succeed, and … build that confidence and momentum.'[20]

Regular small victories have more impact than infrequent big victories. When you kick goals, you feel good. When you feel good, you want to kick more goals. You celebrate the small stuff and enjoy the ride, rather than postponing the celebration to a day in the future when you *might* finally get to that lofty, unrealistic goal. The icing on the cake? By not overcommitting, you avoid the overwhelm and burnout that often creep in when setting new habits.

'Regular small victories have more impact than infrequent big victories. When you kick goals, you feel good.'

Defined, Realistic And Specific

A note on how to frame the goal itself: if your goal is 'to start meditating regularly' that sounds really lovely ... but it's super vague.

So instead, let's make sure your goal is defined, realistic and specific. Bonus points for making it action oriented. As in, 'I will meditate for 10 minutes a day, five days a week, for the next 21 days.' With a goal like that, you have your marching orders. You know exactly what you need to do. Which makes it easier to actually do the damn thing.

Commit To It

Wondering why you should even bother setting a goal or schedule? It's a way of making a commitment. When we commit in earnest to something, it gives us staying power in the process. We agree to show up for it even when it's hard or messy or feels frustrating.

Just as you don't ditch your partner when they irritate the shit out of you by leaving a dirty bowl in the sink, or quit your job because of one annoying email from a client, when you're committed to your meditation practice, you don't abandon it when the going gets tough and your meditation is frustrating AF one day. When the morning is busy or the house is noisy or your mind wanders like a lost dog, you show up anyway because your big-picture commitment to the practice overrides the daily circumstances.

Bottom line: If you want to create change, consistency is key. You *can* change. Shit, your *brain* can change, and I just showed you some research that proves it. But none of the benefits show up if you don't.

Track Star

Once you've set your goal, you may want to track your progress. There are many ways you can do this. Here's a little potpourri of tracking options for your consideration:

❊ Box Ticker

Tick boxes on a calendar or tracking page. Competitive types who love to chase a high score or look at graphs, charts and tangible numbers, this is for you. Try to keep the chain unbroken!

❊ Take Note

Complete a short and sweet journal entry before and after each meditation. This way of tracking gives you insight into how you're feeling before and after your practice, and what's changing over time. It's also a great opportunity to touch base with the Reflection On Your Direction metric from the Worksheet in Chapter 10 (#5, page 170)!

❊ Buddy Up

If social accountability helps you stay on track, share your goal in a public place like Facebook or Instagram and then regularly post your progress. Better yet, get a buddy on board to do it with you. Scoop up some shareable graphics at caitlincady.com/bookbonuses

Once you've been tracking for six months or so and have an established practice, you may find you don't need a tracking system anymore. Once you're truly on the meditation train, you won't want to get off, so it's easy to keep going.

Try This:
DO IT ON THE DAILY

When I was just starting out, my goal was to meditate five to six days a week. But after a short while, I was hooked and started to do it on the daily. Now meditation is just part of my daily routine.

In the same way I don't weigh up whether or not to brush my teeth every morning, I don't debate whether or not I'm going to meditate. I just do the damn thing. I know brushing my teeth is good for my health (and, let's be honest, my social life—morning breath is nobody's friend!).

Similarly, I know that meditation is good for me. I know that when I meditate, I'm happier, more productive, more positive, more present, more patient, and calmer. For those reasons and more, meditation has become a non-negotiable part of my day.

But that's just me. If a daily practice feels like too much to weave into your life initially, don't sweat it. Just commit to a regular schedule—any schedule that feels doable.

WORKSHEET
MEDITATION RX

This worksheet is designed to help you define your personalised prescription for getting Heavily Meditated. (While this is geared toward meditation, you can easily tweak the questions for exercise, yoga, self-care or any other personal practice you'd like to establish in your life. Holla!)

You can also download a printable version of this worksheet at *caitlincady.com/bookbonuses*

Your Personal Starting Point

1. How much time can I realistically devote to a meditation practice on a weekly basis? How many minutes on how many days?

   _____ *days a week for* _____ *minutes*

   SUGGESTIONS:

   3–4 days a week / 10–15 minutes
   5 days a week / 10 minutes
   7 days a week / 5–15 minutes

2. What time of day can I set an appointment with myself to sit and meditate?

   _____

3. Where will I sit?

   _____

4. How long am I willing to commit to this schedule?
   (21 days, 3 months, 6 months, etc.)

   _____

Face Your Resistance

You know all of those objections and obstacles and niggling doubts that are still floating around in your brain-piece? All the reasons you think you can't meditate, or won't stick with it, or won't like it? Let's flip the script on all of those bad boys. By being clear and honest about objections, doubts or past habit-forming fails, you can address them before they have any power at all.

Write down each objection, challenge or obstacle in the first column, and then flip the script in the middle column. Then in the third column, jot down an action step that will help you overcome the hurdle of that particular objection. In terms of action steps, think about what you need to support your practice (e.g. a room with a door, guided meditations, noise-cancelling headphones, asking your partner to watch the kids).

Download online at *caitlincady.com/bookbonuses*

Resistance	Script Flip	Action Step
EXCUSES, FEARS, DOUBTS, ROADBLOCKS	THE SILVER LINING OR THE REFRAME	AN ACTIONABLE SOLUTION
I don't have time.	*Meditation gives me enhanced focus and productivity, which opens up more time in my day.*	*Set my alarm to wake up 15 minutes earlier every morning.*
It hurts my knees to sit cross-legged.	*I've got options! A cushion under my hips will make me more comfy.*	*Set up a Zen Den in the corner of my bedroom with the cushions and bolsters I need to sit comfortably.*

Take Action

Reviewing the Action Step column on the previous page, circle the three most powerful action steps you can take to set yourself up for a consistent daily practice, then write them down here.

1. _____
_____
_____

2. _____
_____
_____

3. _____
_____
_____

Gateway MEDITATION

Remember when we took all those different meditations for a spin? Time to revisit that worksheet. Flip back to Chapter 8 (page 127) and grab the name of your Gateway Meditation. You can either listen to that guided meditation (links at caitlincady.com/bookbonuses), or if you feel confident, use a timer and venture into the technique solo-style. Either way is gravy.

Your Meditation Rx.

Studies show[21] that people who write down their goals accomplish more than those who do not. By a long shot. So let's bring this all together into a clear, written goal. This is your personalised Meditation Prescription to keep you Heavily Meditated on the regular. Print it out, pin it up. Use as directed.

Download a printable version at *caitlincady.com/bookbonuses* ↓

MEDITATION RX.

NAME: _____ DATE: __ / __ / __

DIRECTIONS:

_____ minutes of _____ meditation
                    [GATEWAY MEDITATION NAME]

_____ times per week at _____ for _____ .
                          [MORNING/NIGHT]   [DAYS/WEEKS/MONTHS]

TAKE YOUR MEDS

Enjoy The Buzz.

Next, I'm sharing the secrets on upgrading your meditation from a habit into a lush ritual. Spoiler alert— there's hot fudge and sprinkles involved.

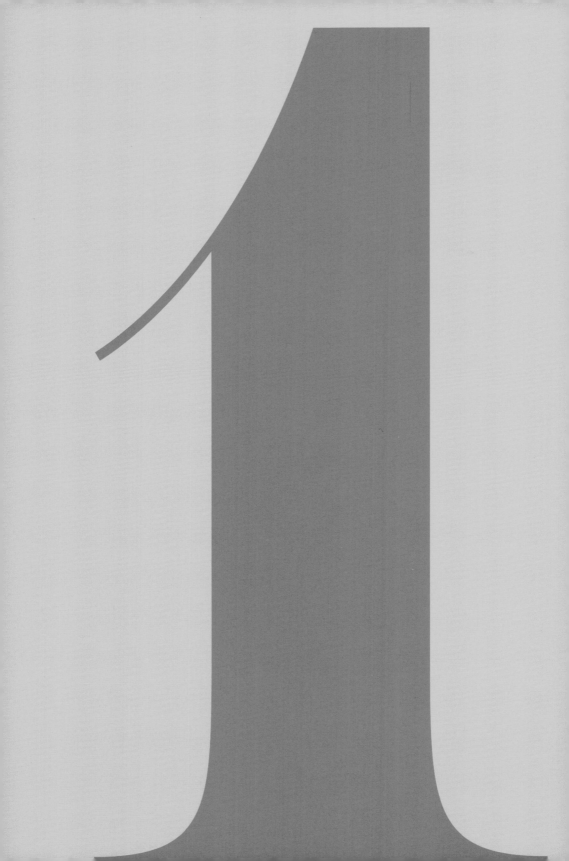

2

Chapter Twelve.

FROM A HABIT TO A
RITUAL: YOUR PRACTICE,
WITH SPRINKLES

UPGRADE YOUR
PRACTICE
FROM A HABIT
TO A RITUAL

My ultimate goal with this book is to help you create a meditation practice that you *love.* Something that *feels good.* Because when something feels good, you will keep coming back for more. One of the ways to up your chances of becoming a meditation junkie is to kit yourself out with some goodies that enhance and expand your practice.

Think of it this way. Meditation itself is the bowl of ice cream (refined-sugar-free-fair-trade-vegan-paleo-coconut-nice-cream, obvi). And what I'm about to suggest are the toppings that turn your bowl of ice cream into a hot fudge sundae with sprinkles.

Look, if you're happy with the bowl of ice cream, I tip my hat to you. The toppings definitely aren't necessary. In fact, meditation purists would probably shudder to hear me comparing meditation to an ice cream sundae. But WHATEVER.

I love the whole idea of expanding and embellishing a daily routine or habit into a *ritual*. A habit sounds not-so-sexy—something you need, but don't want, to do. On the flip side, a ritual sounds inspiring, intentional, uplifting and nourishing. Something you look forward to.

As habit-guru Gretchen Rubin puts it, 'a "routine" is a string of habits, and a "ritual" is a habit charged with transcendent meaning.'[22] Reframing your meditation practice from a *habit* into a *ritual* is a worthy undertaking. So, I've gathered up a few upgrades you might like to integrate into your meditation practice. These can enhance your experience, making you fall even more deeply in love with your meditation practice. On a sensory level, these upgrades can also send a signal to your brain that it's time to meditate or leverage those post-meditation highs to make some magic. Without further ado, I present ... all the toppings.

Go Smudge Yourself

One of my favourite ways to begin any ritual, including meditation, is to clear the energy with the smoke from dried sage leaves or other herbs and plants. (And no, cannabis doesn't count, yo, so you can put your pipe away.) Smudging is an ancient cleansing technique for removing negativity. It's a ceremonial way to say 'Bye, Felicia' to bad vibes.

If that sounds a little out there, try this on for size. *The Journal of Ethnopharmacology* has published papers[23] on the effectiveness of smudging in purifying the air, and even changing the molecular structure of the air. Plus, the negative ions in the smoke are believed to boost mood and dispel bad vibes.

I like to use a bundle of white sage (purifying and protective), a braid of dried sweetgrass (unifying and calming), or a stick of palo santo (brings good fortune and enhances creativity). To clear the air, light the smudge stick, let the flame burn out, and use your hand or a feather to fan the embers and move the smoke around your entire body, moving top to toe, visualising the smoke dissolving any negative energy and surrounding you with good vibes.

You might like to whisper a little invocation as you go. Borrow these or create your own ... 'In this smoke, all attachments and dark energetic thought forms are cleansed and cleared. All that remains are the most loving expressions of the highest vibrations. I am light and love. And so it is.' Or, sing along to 'Burn baby burn, disco inferno!' Whatever feels right.

'Burn baby burn, disco inferno!'

Good Vibes (And Negative Ions) Only

Another option is to light up a beeswax candle and let it burn while you meditate. The subtle honey scent is heavenly, but beeswax candles bring more than a sweet smell to the party. Pure beeswax candles are non-toxic, and actually emit negative ions. And negative ions make us feel good. You know how you feel after you've had some hang time by the ocean? Yep, that air is chock-full of negative ions.

'Negative ions make us feel good.'

But even better, the negative ions emitted by the candles bind with toxins, allergens and pollutants to improve air quality. So all your deep, full-belly meditation breaths will be toxin-free and infused with good vibes.

TRY THIS: THE BEE'S KNEES

FYI: all candles are not created equal. Ditch your regular candles for some beeswax ones, STAT. Sad but true: most candles are made from paraffin wax, filled with artificial colours and synthetic fragrances, and have wicks laden with heavy metals. This all adds up to a toxic brew that can damage the brain, central nervous system and lungs, and can contribute to illnesses ranging from allergies to cancer. No thanks.

Even the 'natural' soy wax candles are problematic. Most soy wax candles aren't made from 100 per cent soy (yep, paraffin is often lurking behind misleading labels!). Further to that, candles scented with essential oils aren't always ideal. Some essential oils become toxic when burned. Your best bet is 100 per cent pure, unscented beeswax candles with cotton wicks. If you want, you can pair the candle with some pure organic essential oils and a diffuser for a winning combo that won't do a number on your lungs.

Get Stoned

As energetic beings, we're in a constant state of vibration and can be easily thrown off course, out of balance, or into a state of dis-ease due to the constant influx of energies and vibrations we encounter. Think EMFs (electromagnetic fields) and just ... you know, your run-of-the-mill energy vampire type of people.

One tool you can use to keep the good vibes flowing is crystals. The historical use of crystals for health, protection and healing exists in a vast array of ancient traditions from Greece to India, Egypt to China, Australia to the Americas. Crystals are millions of years old, forged during the earth's formation, and are considered to be the most orderly structure in nature. They respond to energy inputs around them by transforming and harmonising the energy, and they are also capable of storing information.

According to *The Book of Stones* by Robert Simmons and Naisha Ahsian, 'when we bring the crystal into our electromagnetic field, two things occur. The electromagnetic frequencies carried by the stone will vibrate with related frequencies in our own energy field through the physical law of resonance, creating a third larger vibration field. The nervous system is attuned to these shifts in energy and transmits this information to the brain. Here the frequencies stimulate biochemical shifts that affect the physical body and shift brain function.'[24]

Crystals create a sense of harmony and can enhance intentions and manifest particular energies. By regularly meditating with a particular crystal, you balance your energy and simultaneously infuse the crystal with your meditative vibes. The crystal then becomes a touchstone (yes, pun intended) for staying aligned with that meditative energy, or with your intention. I'm no crystal expert, but here are three common crystals that can be useful in meditation:

✳ Clear quartz, also known as the 'master healer' (how's that for a job title?), is believed to amplify thoughts and work wonders for manifestation.

✳ Rose quartz, known as the stone of love, harmony and positivity.

✳ Amethyst, to connect with intuition and support mental clarity.

Aromatic Anchors

Essential oils can serve as aromatic anchors to help you drop into meditation more quickly. The beautiful smells are pleasure-inducing and grounding. You can also select an essential oil related to your intention. For example, peppermint oil can perk up your brain, sandalwood can help you feel more grounded, and lavender will help you chillax. Check the Resources section for a few of my favourite oils and where to get them.

To use the oils, you can either use an ultrasonic diffuser, which uses ultrasonic waves and water to disperse essential oils into the air as negative ions. Or simply apply a drop of oil into your palms, rub them together, open your palms, and inhale deeply!

Another option is to use a mist that incorporates essential oils, flower essences and crystal codes. My favourites are Shemana Elixirs. These mists combine botanical bodaciousness and natural nourishment to enhance your intentions and create magical meditations. Check the Resources section for details.

Set The Mood

Reading a page or two from an inspiring book can be a nice way to set the mood for meditation or to wrap it up. A gorgeous poem, an uplifting bit of prose or a thoughtful spiritual snippet can give some direction for your day, offer you something meaningful to contemplate or simply add a bit of beauty to your world. Check the Resources section for a short list of some of my most dog-eared paperbacks.

Take Notes

Ending your meditation with a short journalling session is a good way to close your practice and record any insights that came up. The quantity and quality of solutions, insights, inspirations and ideas that will come to you through meditation are quite astounding. Word to the wise: jot them down as soon as you wrap up your practice. I find if I don't document these downloads straight away, they tend to vanish without a trace.

TRY THIS: BRAIN DUMP

Another way to integrate pen and paper into your practice is to do a bit of a brain dump right before you meditate. It gives you the opportunity to put to paper all the niggling little to-dos and must-remembers and don't-forgets. If you're a list lover then this could be a good strategy to employ as it will give you a sense of freedom and space when you begin your meditation practice.

'The quantity and quality of solutions, insights, inspirations and ideas that will come to you through meditation are quite astounding.'

Get Grateful

While you've got your journal out, jot down what you're grateful for on that particular day. I love happiness expert Shawn Achor's approach to gratitude. He suggests writing down three things for which you're grateful from the last 24 hours. This is super powerful for a few reasons.

First, it can be really easy to slip into a gratitude rut, repeating the same 'big' things every day ('my health, my family' etc.). Using Achor's approach keeps your gratitude fresh and relevant and brings your attention to the little bijoux in your day, the tiny gems that you might otherwise miss. You keep your eyes peeled, so to speak, for all the many blessings in your life.

Plus, this consistent attitude of gratitude expands and sets you up to receive even more to be grateful for. As Dr Habib Sadhegi says, 'feeling is the language of the universe',[25] so generating feelings of gratitude and recognising all your gifts and blessings invites more of the good stuff into your life. In other words, *thank you* and *please* go hand in hand. So go forth and be grateful.

GO FORTH
go forth

AND BE
and be

GRATEFUL.
grateful

Mention Your Intention

Intention is the creative power we hold in manifesting our dreams and desires, big or small. In the *The Upanishads* (an ancient Vedic text from India), it is written, 'you are what your deepest desire is. As your desire is, so is your intention. As your intention is, so is your will. As your will is, so is your deed. As your deed is, so is your destiny.'

When you set an intention based on your desires, it guides you to act in alignment with the desire. Put another way, setting an intention is a way to generate your state. Post meditation is prime time to mention your intention. You're calm, clear and focused. If you meditate in the morning, even better. An intention can set the tone for your whole day and act as a compass, steering you toward the next right step.

> 'When you set an intention based on your desires, it guides you to act in alignment with the desire.'

To set an intention, sense what your deepest desire is, either for the day or the bigger picture of your life. Then set an intention centred around that.

The affirmation you created in Chapter 10 (specifically in #6 (page 171) in the Map To What Matters Worksheet) would make a perfect intention! Alternatively, if you want to set a more specific intention for your day, here are a few ideas that you might want to adopt or adapt.

Note: I like to work in feelings, so I usually zone in on two or three words or a short phrase that points to the feels and qualities I want to embody for the day.[26]

Desire	Intention
Harmonious relationships.	*Let me be an ocean of understanding.*
Invoking inspiration and creativity.	*Receptivity, eloquence, fluency, grace.*
To feel nourished and rested.	*Slow and steady. Nourished, radiant and receptive.*
To complete a big creative or work project.	*I flow forward with focus, ease and grace.*
To feel happy.	*I find the spark of joy in all things. I fan the flames and let them spread like wildfire.*
To make big decisions with ease.	*I trust myself. I let my heart lead the way.*
To show up fully present with my loved ones.	*I am filled with pure presence and the bliss of being in the here and now.*
To create abundance.	*I receive with ease and gratitude. I am open to abundance.*

Once you're clear on your intention, focus on the intention for a few moments, repeating it in your mind. Visualise yourself moving through your day with this intention in action. Imagine that the intention becomes reality and sense how that feels in your body and heart. You might like to write down your intention in a place where you'll see it throughout the day.

Jam Session

If you're musically minded, integrate a set of chimes, tingshaws, gong or singing bowl into your practice. It's a groovy way to mark the beginning and end of your practice. These instruments are, by nature, ritualistic objects. Their sounds are purifying and harmonising, and can actually affect your brainwaves.

On a basic level, the ringing of a chime, gong or bowl can act as a summons, bringing you into the present moment and creating a sacred space. On days when you have time for an extra lush meditation, feel free to have a little jam session for a few minutes at the end of your meditation. If you have kids, this is a fun way to include them in your practice. My kids love playing the singing bowl or ringing the gong and feeling the sounds vibrate through their bodies.

Pick A Card

One of my favourite toppings on a super deluxe meditation sundae is pulling an oracle or tarot card. If it's a special occasion (hey birthday girl), a lunar event (like a full moon or new moon), or even if you just need a dose of guidance or clarity, get out the deck. Pulling cards at the end of a meditation is the perfect time because you're in a calm, clear, receptive headspace.

Tarot and oracle cards represent archetypes and universal truths. They help us dig deep and tap into our intuition and subconscious mind. Through synchronicity (the belief and trust that we pull a particular card for a reason) and symbolism (the universal truth and meaning of each card), we can access our inner knowing, gain a deeper understanding, and garner insight so that we can move forward with clarity. It's sometimes eerie how on point the card is. Give it a try and see what you think. (Pssst ... I've given a shout out to my favourite card deck in the Resources section.)

So there you have it. Alllll the toppings for a truly transcendent ritual. Grab a spoon and decorate that meditation sundae to your liking— and then dig in with gusto.

Excuse Buster

YOUR QUICK GUIDE
TO DEBUNKING
MEDITATION MYTHS
& EXCUSES

I've got your back.

IF YOU FIND THAT YOU'RE TALKING YOURSELF OUT OF MEDITATION (WHICH YOU WILL, IT'S ONLY NORMAL), I'VE GOT YOU COVERED. COME BACK TO THIS EXCUSE BUSTER ANYTIME YOU NEED A LITTLE KICK IN THE PANTS.

❋ OOPS. I FAFFED AROUND ON INSTAGRAM FOR AN HOUR AND NOW I'VE RUN OUT OF TIME TO MEDITATE!

The average person spends one to three hours on social media. A DAY. Which translates to brain-drain and a diluted sense of self. If you choose to redirect that energy and spend even an eighth of the time spent scrolling the 'gram meditating instead, you will feel enlivened, energised, clear and creative. Flip your status update from 'Dazed & Confused' to 'Heavily Meditated' in as little as 10 minutes. I'll thumbs up and double tap to that.

❋ I DON'T BELIEVE IN MEDITATION.

Meditation isn't Santa Claus or the Tooth Fairy or a magic trick or a religion. It's not something you *have* to *believe* in, have faith in, or even understand. All you have to do is be open to it and be willing to witness the proof of your personal experience. If you stick with meditation, the outcomes speak for themselves.

❋ I FEEL SUPER GUILTY SITTING HERE AND DOING NOTHING. ISN'T THIS KIND OF SELF-INDULGENT?

Do you feel guilty when you take time to exercise? Or when you take a shower or eat a nourishing meal? Probably not. So why would you feel guilty when you meditate? Meditation is an investment, not an indulgence. It's an investment in your wellbeing, and it pays dividends for you and for all of those who cross your path. Meditation falls into the category of the most fundamental forms of self-care. As they say, you can't pour from an empty cup. Further to that, when you heal your shit, you heal the world. So stop shaming yourself for looking after yourself. BTW, if you have little ones, hear this: it's your *duty* to set an example of exceptional self-care. Teach them well.

✳ BUT I'M NOT LIKE YOU. MY MIND IS LOOSE AF.

Dude. I get it. I promise. I've been meditating for years and I still find myself lost in thought. But I don't get my undies in a bunch, chuck my toys, or throw in the towel. I just return my attention back to the focal point, as many times as it takes. 'Cause that's the whole point. Meditation sit-ups, bro.

✳ IT'S TOO HARD TO SIT STILL RIGHT NOW.

Ahhh, yes, our old friend, resistance. That punk has been ruining meditations since time immemorial. Usually, we're avoiding stillness because there's something uncomfortable waiting for us there. So ask yourself: what feeling am I afraid to feel? When you have your answer, sit and feel it and see what happens.

✳ MEDITATION SUCKS.

True, there are some truly horrendous guided meditations out there on the interwebs. To be honest, if I'd heard those as my first experience with meditation I would have said a resounding, 'Oh. Hell. No.' and promptly headed for the couch to binge watch *Billions* and drink a bottle of rosé. But here's the beauty of it. Just as there is a teacher for every student, there's a meditation for every mind. It's not a one-size-fits-all thing. What works for you might not work for your sister. What works for you today might not be your jam in three months. And what you totally *don't* dig today might be your little piece of brain bliss tomorrow. So be open. Be playful. Shake it up. Experiment and find what works for you.

❄ I DON'T HAVE TIME.

Nobody has the time. You make the time. We are all given the same 24 hours in a day, boo. If Madonna, Oprah, Tim Ferriss, Arianna Huffington, Kate Hudson and Kobe Bryant have time to meditate, pretty sure there is some crafty way that you can sneak a few minutes of meditation into your day, too. And if you're too busy to meditate, then maybe you're just too busy, full stop. If that's the case, it's time to reclaim your life.

❄ I CAN'T STOP THINKING.

No worries. You don't need to! Remember that you've spent your whole life identifying with your thoughts. That's not going to change overnight. But as you practise meditation, you practise creating space between you and your thoughts—as well as allowing space between the thoughts themselves. As you create more space, you'll shake up the patterns and conditioning of your habitual thoughts and behaviours. You'll let a little light in. Little by little. Day by day. Sit by sit.

❄ I MISSED A MEDITATION, SO NOW IT'S ALL RUINED.

Missing a meditation happens once in a while. Don't stress, just get back on the wagon as soon as you can. Meditation has a cumulative effect, which is why it's so useful to do it on the regular. Every time you make a deposit in the meditation bank, you boost presence, you increase clarity, you fortify yourself against crumbling to cravings or angry outbursts. Over time you'll find that you're less likely to succumb to reactivity because you have a savings account of meditation moolah stacked up for a rainy day like this.

❋ I ONLY HAVE FIVE MINUTES.

Even a few minutes of meditation are better than none. As the guru to The Beatles and The Beach Boys, Maharishi Mahesh Yogi, is reported to have said, 'even in a shallow dive we get wet.' Start with five minutes and I bet you'll be deep-diving in no time.

❋ I FORGOT.

You're cute. Hot tip: do it at the same time every day. This makes it a basically unforgettable habit. And if that fails, set a calendar reminder. Hint: make it playful. Like '7:45 am LEVITATE.' Or '8 pm GET SIT DONE.' If it makes you smile, you'll create a positive association, which will keep you coming back for more.

meditation is
an investment,
not an insurance

tion is

stment,

dulgence.

Resources

INFORMATION,
TOOLS & GOODIES

❋ GUIDED MEDITATIONS

HEAVILY MEDITATED

caitlincady.com

Yep, that's me! Here you'll find a variety of guided meditations (including the five companion meditations for this book), in addition to other helpful resources and inspiration.

YOGARUPA ROD STRYKER

glo.com or parayoga.com

My yoga and meditation teacher. An incredible 'living link' to ancient wisdom of tantra and heath yoga. Rod's 'Four Desires' meditations (available via his website or his app, Sanctuary) are some of my all-time favourite guided meditations. These meditations are rooted in spiritual traditions but they feel very practical and grounded.

SALLY KEMPTON

glo.com or sallykempton.com

A highly regarded teacher of meditation and spiritual philosophy who spent 20 years as a teaching swami (monk). Her meditations may be a good fit for you if you're more spiritually inclined, and if mantra and visualisation are your jam.

TARA JUDELLE

glo.com

A yoga teacher (and student of Sally Kempton's). Her meditations often involve awareness of the various organs and systems within the body, so if body scans and awareness meditation speak to you, Tara's meditations would be a nice pick.

TARA BRACH

tarabrach.com or through her eponymous podcast

Tara blends Western psychology with Eastern spiritual practices. Her talks and meditations are incredibly approachable, relatable and inviting. The Buddhist roots of Tara's shine through in the way she weaves wisdom and compassion into her meditations. If awareness meditation (like body scans) or watching the breath works well for you, give Tara's meditations a try.

INSIGHT TIMER APP

insighttimer.com

This free app offers timer functions for self-guided meditations as well as a wide variety of guided meditations, including some by yours truly!

HEADSPACE APP

headspace.com

If you'd prefer to steer clear of spiritual references altogether, Headspace might be a good fit for you. The meditations are pared back with no music and simple instructions.

❋ MEDITATION MUSIC

SACRED ACOUSTICS

sacredacoustics.com

Both guided and unguided (my preference) tracks are available. If you dig meditation on sound, take these for a spin.

✳ MEDITATION TOOLS

PURE PRANA LABEL MEDITATION CUSHIONS

purepranalabel.com

These are beautiful handmade, eco-friendly cushions. I go for
the round cushion in standard height (12 cm). Cindy will make you
a custom cushion, too!

CLAY TWOMBLY MALA BEADS

claytwombly.com

These beautiful malas are handmade by Clay on Nantucket using
semi-precious gemstones, crystals, and sandalwood beads.

LAMBSKIN RUG

ecowool.com

I place my meditation cushion on top of a lambskin rug. I recommend
seeking out an eco-friendly option that doesn't use harsh chemicals like
arsenic and formaldehyde in the tanning process. My pick is the Ecowool
Sheepskin Baby Rug.

NOISE-CANCELLING HEADPHONES

bose.com

I use Bose Quiet Comfort 35 Headphones. These noise-cancelling
beauties are a dream for guided meditations or listening to
meditation music.

❊ MEDITATION TOPPINGS

TAROT/ORACLE CARDS

There are a myriad of options out there, so it's best to pop into your local bookstore and have a play with a deck or two to see which ones resonate with you! Here are a couple of my favourites:

Kuan Yin Oracle by Alana Fairchild

These are beautifully illustrated and the messages are so gorgeous. Always my favourite choice. This deck comes with a little companion book that offers insight into the symbolism of each card and a prayer to recite if you choose.

Truthbomb Card Decks by Danielle LaPorte

Short, snappy stand-alone messages that are always on point, these are sort of like a modern-day oracle. More literal than symbolic, these cards don't come with a companion book of explanations, but they are succinct and beautiful enough to prop up on your desk or dresser.

ESSENTIAL OILS

livinglibations.com

I buy my essential oils from Living Libations. The quality and integrity of the products are excellent. My favourite blends are Jasmine Julep (so uplifting), Love Wine (nice in a bath or a hot chocolate!), and Laurel Oracle (ace for focus!). Other basics that are good to have on hand are lavender (relaxation), peppermint (puts a literal pep in your step), citruses like blood orange or grapefruit (uplifting and cheerful), or sandalwood (earthy and grounding). And of course, I can't go past my favourite, rose otto. It's indulgent, but a drop in the diffuser is heaven on earth.

SHEMANA CRYSTALLINE ELIXIR MISTS

shemana.com.au

I just can't get enough of these mists which are pure aromatherapy botanicals activated with crystals and wildflowers. The Crystal Clearing mist is perfect for preparing for meditation (I also spritz it at my desk when I need a fresh start). The Heart Mist is my favourite. But I also keep the Savasana and Dream Mists on hand at all times!

BEESWAX CANDLES

queenb.com.au or northernlight.com.au

Always look for 100 per cent beeswax candles without colours or scents.

❋ INSPIRING AND UPLIFTING POST-MEDITATION READS

Prayers for Honoring by Pixie Lighthorse

Prayers for Honoring Voice by Pixie Lighthorse

The Radiance Sutras by Lorin Roche, PhD

The Essential Rumi translation by Coleman Barks

The Four Agreements by Don Miguel Ruiz

Women Who Run with the Wolves by Clarissa Pinkola Estés

A Return to Love by Marianne Williamson

Braving the Wilderness by Brené Brown

Big Magic by Elizabeth Gilbert

Ask and It Is Given by Esther Hicks and Jerry Hicks

A Course in Miracles Made Easy by Alan Cohen

The Alchemist by Paulo Coelho

✳ OTHER RESOURCES

THE ACT MATRIX

drkevinpolk.com

Dr Kevin Polk's ACT Matrix is an incredibly useful tool, parts of which I borrowed (with his generous permission) in the Map To What Matters Most worksheet in this book.

SHAWN ACHOR

goodthinkinc.com

The positive psychology guru!

THE DESIRE MAP BOOK

amazon.com

The Desire Map: A Guide to Creating Goals with Soul by Danielle LaPorte offers up a powerful process for getting clear about what you most deeply desire (how you want to feel), so you can then set goals that move you closer to those feelings.

❊ ENDNOTES

1   Chödrön, P. *When Things Fall Apart: Heart Advice for Difficult Times* (Anniversary ed.). Boulder, Shambhala, 2016.

2   Kempton, S. 'Life Questions.' https://www.sallykempton.com/resources/life-questions/

3   Sadeghi, H. *Within: A Spiritual Awakening to Love and Weight Loss.* New York, Open Road Media, 2014.

4   Stryker, R. *The Art and Science of Practice.* Creature Yoga, 10 February 2017.

5   Taren, AA, Creswell, JD, and Gianaros, PJ. 'Dispositional mindfulness co-varies with smaller amygdala and caudate volumes in community adults.' 2013. http://journals.plos.org/plosone/article?id=10.1371/journal.pone.0064574

6   Hölzel, BK, Carmody, J, Vangel, M, Congleton, C, Yerramsetti,SM, Gard, T, and Lazar, SW. 'Mindfulness practice leads to increases in regional brain gray matter density.' 2010. https://www.ncbi.nlm.nih.gov/pmc/articles/PMC3004979

7   Weaver, L. 'The pace of modern life versus our cavewoman biochemistry: Dr Libby Weaver at TedxQueenstown.' TEDxQueenstown, February 2014.

8   Harte, JL, Eifert, GH, and Smith, R. 'The effects of running and meditation on beta-endorphin, corticotropin-releasing hormone and cortisol in plasma, and on mood.' 1995. http://www.sciencedirect.com/science/article/pii/030105119505118T

9   Ophir, E, Nass, C, and Wagner, AD. 'Cognitive control in media multitaskers.' 2009. http://www.pnas.org/content/106/37/15583.short

10   Foerde, K, Knowlton, BJ, and Poldrack, RA. 'Modulation of competing memory systems by distraction.' 2006. http://www.pnas.org/content/103/31/11778.full

11   Pagnoni, G. 'Dynamical properties of BOLD activity from the ventral posteromedial cortex associated with meditation and attentional skills.' 2012. http://www.jneurosci.org/content/32/15/5242.full.pdf

12   Hagen, S. *Meditation Now or Never.* New York, HarperOne, 2007.

13   Estés, CP. *Women Who Run with the Wolves: Myths and Stories of the Wild Woman Archetype.* New York, Ballantine, 1995.

14   Weil, S. *First and Last Notebooks.* London; New York, Oxford University Press, 1970.

15   Hölzel, BK, Carmody, J, Vangel, M, Congleton, C, Yerramsetti, SM, Gard, T, and Lazar, SW. 'Mindfulness practice leads to increases in regional brain gray matter density.' 2010. https://www.ncbi.nlm.nih.gov/pmc/articles/PMC3004979/

16   Side note: Maureen Dowd's Op Ed 'Valley of the rolls' is worth a read. Funny, and a little scary. https://www.nytimes.com/2006/03/18/opinion/valley-of-the-rolls.html

17   Black, DS, O'Reilly, GA, Olmstead, R, Breen, EC, and Irwin, MR. 'Mindfulness meditation and improvement in sleep quality and daytime impairment among older adults with sleep disturbances.' 2015. https://jamanetwork.com/journals/jamainternalmedicine/fullarticle/2110998

18   Shout out to psychologist Dr Kevin Polk! This process is a spin on his ACT Matrix. If you dig this methodology, check him out on YouTube or on his website, http://www.drkevinpolk.com/

19   Robinson, R. 'The Tim Ferriss approach to setting goals: Rig the game so you win.' *Entrepreneur*, 5 May 2016. https://www.entrepreneur.com/article/275124

20   Ibid.

21   Murphy, M. 'Neuroscience explains why you need to write down your goals if you actually want to achieve them.' *Forbes*, 15 April 2018. https://www.forbes.com/sites/markmurphy/2018/04/15/neuroscience-explains-why-you-need-to-write-down-your-goals-if-you-actually-want-to-achieve-them/

22   Rubin, G. *Better than Before: Mastering the Habits of Our Everyday Lives*. New York, Crown, 2015.

23   Nautiyal CS, Chauhan PS, and Nene YL. 'Medicinal smoke reduces airborne bacteria.' 2007. https://www.ncbi.nlm.nih.gov/pubmed/17913417#

24   Simmons, R, Ahsian, N, and Raven, H. *The Book of Stones: Who They Are and What They Teach*. East Montpelier, Heaven & Earth Publishing, 2015.

25   Sadeghi, H. *Within: A Spiritual Awakening to Love and Weight Loss*. New York, Open Road Media, 2014.

26   If you're a fan of working with the feels, check out Danielle LaPorte's book *The Desire Map*.

POWER TO THE PEACEFUL.

Gratitudes and Acknowledgements

To my husband, Loren. I hit the jackpot with you, dude. Thank you for your strength, your steadiness and your sweetness. Thank you for wrangling the babies while I meditate every morning. Thank you for giving me the grace and space to write amidst the mayhem. Thank you for your faith in me and for always having my back. Thank you for co-creating this extraordinary life with me. I carry your heart ...

To my babies, Oliver, Isla and Hanalei. Thank you for teaching me about life and love. Thank you for evolving me. Thank you for giving me a reason to refine myself. Thank you for the inspiration you offer just by being. Humbled and honoured by each of you, sweet babies.

To my mama, Lisa. You gave me agency over my own life and that is the greatest gift any parent can give their child. Thank you for saying yes to every single dream I've ever had. Thank you for instilling me with the creativity and self-belief to dream big and the determination to actually get shit done. Thank you for teaching me how to love fiercely and live stylishly. Thank you for making life magic for me.

To my papa, Tracey. Thank you for endowing me with a love of the written word. For writing and drawing with me when I was only knee-high, for telling stories by the fire, and for reading books in bed. Thank you for introducing me to Siddhartha and Gandhi and e.e. and Mary. Thank you for always seeing the best in me and for encouraging me to let my heart lead the way.

To the people who have knowingly or unknowingly taught me about meditation, who have expanded my inner horizons, and have guided me back to the divinity within, I bow to you. Yogarupa Rod Stryker, Sally Kempton, Dr Tara Brach, Dr Scott Lyons, Jane Hardwicke Collings, Dr Clarissa Pinkola Estés ... I'm forever grateful to you and your work.

To my former work-wife and life-long love Brieann Boal, I'll never be able to thank you enough for dragging me out from behind the curtain. You gave me permission and a place to shine and I'll never stop thanking you.

To Sally for being the most sacred sounding board. For patiently reading and re-reading. For helping me to refine. For your incredible presence. For your text messages and love letters that gave me wings when I was feeling afraid to fly. Thank you for seeing me, sis.

To Dr Monica Taylor for sharing your time and talent to patiently translate the headiest medical terminology and high-brow science into something a regular gal could make sense of. You amaze me. Perpetually. Love your bones, GF.

To my tribe of kindreds near and far—hot damn, I f*ckin love you. Thank you for being my people. Monifa, Meagsy, Soph, Dana, Kim, Foofs, Tyn, Anna, Geraldine, Hayles, Ness, The Shield, Mich, Richie, Dave, Waxy, Jess, Bess. Blessed. By. You.

To my beloved Aunts and Other Mothers who inspire me with their generosity and grace and are always there to cheer me on ... Marki, Tara, Buss, Bern, Woody and Heidi, I love you.

Deep bow to the magical creatures Lala and Mimi who have kept the wildlings loved up and the laundry folded while I write. Thank you for being surrogate sisters to me.

To the incredible circle of creatives that I'm fortunate enough to work with, wow. How did I get so lucky? Bayleigh Vedelago, thank you for making so much visual magic with me ... and for teaching me how to *not* be a hot mess in front of the camera. Dani and Elle at Neverland, thank you for bringing my vision to life, and for always elevating my words with your mad design skills. To my right-hand woman, soul sis', spreadsheet wizard, logistical genie and all-round legend Tyneal Alexander, thank you for your careful attention, for seeing the big picture and managing the small details, but most of all for your grace. To my developmental editor Laura Lee Mattingly, thank you for helping me polish this book into something I'm proud of. You made me a better writer in the process. Grateful for your editorial expertise, your keen eye for detail, and especially for your warmth and generosity. To my copyeditor Emily Han, thank you for your precision, patience and diligence. So grateful to be surrounded by so many dynamic women. The future really is female.

To the team at Hardie Grant, thank you for making such beautiful books and for giving authors like me a way to reach the world without compromising on creativity. A very special, heartfelt thank you to my publisher, Jane Willson, for believing in me and backing this book. Thank you for your vision and willingness to do things a little differently. I'm humbled, honoured, and forever grateful for the opportunity you've given me to bring my dreams to life.

And most of all, to you, the reader. Thank you. Your eyes on these words are the reason I'm here. It's a privilege and I'm grateful.

Thank you

Medical Disclaimer

While basic meditation is safe for the general population, the practices described in this book do not take into account the reader's individual health, medical, physical, psychological or emotional situation or needs and therefore may not be safe for all people.

The information provided in this book is designed to provide helpful information on the subjects discussed. The author and publisher are not medical professionals and cannot give medical advice or diagnosis. This book is not meant to be used, nor should it be used, to diagnose or treat any medical condition. The reader should, before acting or using any of this information, consider the appropriateness of this information having regard to their own personal situation and needs. For diagnosis or treatment of any medical problem, the reader must consult a medical professional.

The author and publisher expressly disclaim all and any liability to any person in respect of anything and of the consequences of anything done or omitted to be done by any person in reliance, whether in whole or part, upon the whole or any part of the contents of this book and/or any website(s) referred to in it.

Nothing in this medical disclaimer will limit any liabilities of the author or publisher in any way that is prohibited by law, or exclude any liabilities that may not be excluded by law. If anything in this disclaimer is unenforceable, illegal, or void, it is severed and the rest of the disclaimer remains in force.

References are provided for informational purposes only and do not constitute endorsement of any websites or other sources.

Quality Of Content

While the information provided in this book has been prepared and presented with all due care, neither the author nor publisher warrant or represent that the information is free from errors or omission. Neither the author nor the publisher provide any guarantee of the accuracy or currency of any information provided by other parties and referred to within this book.

About The Author
HOPE DEALER, MEDITATION JUNKIE, GANGSTER OF LOVE

Caitlin Cady has been called a 'wellbeing whiz' by *Australian Yoga Journal* and her positive perspectives and relatable, playful approach have inspired people across the globe to get lit up and live to their full potential. American by birth, Caitlin now lives in Byron Bay, Australia with her husband and their three children. When she's not meditating, you can find her hanging at the beach with her family, having a 90s hip hop dance party in her kitchen, or cracking jokes over matcha lattes with her mates.

CONNECT WITH CAITLIN:
INSTAGRAM: @CAITLINCADY | CAITLINCADY.COM

Published in 2020 by Hardie Grant Books,
an imprint of Hardie Grant Publishing

Hardie Grant Books (Melbourne)
Building 1, 658 Church Street
Richmond, Victoria 3121

Hardie Grant Books (London)
5th & 6th Floors
52–54 Southwark Street
London SE1 1UN

hardiegrantbooks.com

 A catalogue record for this
book is available from the
National Library of Australia

Heavily Meditated
ISBN 978 1 74379 614 6

10 9 8 7 6 5 4 3

Publishing Director: Jane Willson
Editors: Laura Lee Mattingly & Emily Han
Design Manager: Jessica Lowe
Designer: Neverland Studio
Photographer: Bayleigh Vedelago
Stylist: Caitlin Cady Nowland
Production Manager: Todd Rechner
Production Coordinator: Mietta Yans

Colour reproduction by Splitting Image Colour Studio
Printed in China by Leo Paper Products LTD.